UNDERSTANDING
TIM O'BRIEN

Understanding Contemporary
American Literature
Matthew J. Bruccoli, General Editor

Volumes on

Edward Albee • John Barth • Donald Barthelme
The Beats • The Black Mountain Poets
Robert Bly • Raymond Carver
Chicano Literature • Contemporary American Drama
Contemporary American Science Fiction
James Dickey • E. L. Doctorow • John Gardner
George Garrett • John Hawkes • Joseph Heller
John Irving • Randall Jarrell • William Kennedy
Ursula K. Le Guin • Denise Levertov • Bernard Malamud
Carson McCullers • Vladimir Nabokov • Joyce Carol Oates
Tim O'Brien • Cynthia Ozick • Walker Percy
Katherine Anne Porter • Thomas Pynchon • Theodore Roethke
Philip Roth • Mary Lee Settle • Isaac Bashevis Singer
Gary Snyder • William Stafford • Anne Tyler
Kurt Vonnegut • Tennessee Williams

UNDERSTANDING
Tim
O'BRIEN

by STEVEN KAPLAN

UNIVERSITY OF SOUTH CAROLINA PRESS

Published in Columbia, South Carolina, by the
University of South Carolina Press

Manufactured in the United States of America

Library of Congress Cataloging-in-Publication Data

Kaplan, Steven, 1953–
    Understanding Tim O'Brien / by Steven Kaplan.
        p.   cm. — (Understanding contemporary American literature)
    Includes bibliographical references and index.
    ISBN 1–57003–007–3
    1. O'Brien, Tim, 1946–   —Criticism and interpretation.
  I. Title. II. Series.
  PS3565.B75Z75   1994   94–3203
  813'.54—dc20

*For my mother
who taught me to value the imagined
and
for Anemone and our children
Aljoscha, Silia, Noemi, and Janina
who have such powerful imaginations*

CONTENTS

The volumes of *Understanding Contemporary American Literature* have been planned as guides or companions for students as well as good nonacademic readers. The editor and publisher perceive a need for these volumes because much of the influential contemporary literature makes special demands. Uninitiated readers encounter difficulty in approaching works that depart from the traditional forms and techniques of prose and poetry. Literature relies on conventions, but the conventions keep evolving; new writers form their own conventions—which in time may become familiar. Put simply, *UCAL* provides instruction in how to read certain contemporary writers—identifying and explicating their material, themes, use of language, point of view, structures, symbolism, and responses to experience.

The word *understanding* in the titles was deliberately chosen. Many willing readers lack an adequate understanding of how contemporary literature works; that is, what the author is attempting to express and the means by which it is conveyed. Although the criticism and analysis in the series have been aimed at a level of general accessibility, these introductory volumes are meant to be applied in conjunction with the works they cover. They do not provide a substitute for the works and authors they introduce, but rather prepare the reader for more profitable literary experiences.

M. J. B.

ACKNOWLEDGMENTS

Passages from the following works by Tim O'Brien reprinted by permission: *If I Die in a Combat Zone, Box Me up and Ship Me Home* (1989, Delta/Seymour Lawrence), *Northern Lights* (1975, Delacorte/Seymour Lawrence), *Going After Cacciato* (1989, Delta/Seymour Lawrence), *The Nuclear Age* (1985, Alfred A. Knopf), *The Things They Carried* (1990, Houghton Mifflin), and *In the Lake of the Woods* (1994, Houghton Mifflin). Special thanks to the managing editor of *Critique* for permission to reprint portions of an article on *The Things They Carried* which appeared in the fall 1993 issue.

The University of Southern Colorado Scholarly Grant Program provided partial funding and release time for this project. I would like to thank Dr. Friederike Wiedemann, Dean of the College of Humanities and Social Sciences at Southern Colorado, for her continual support and encouragement. I would also like to thank the following past and present administrators at the University for their support of my research: Dr. Robert Shirley, Dr. Bruce Grube, and Dr. Keith Lovin. I have found the academic environment at Southern Colorado very conducive to doing research, and this has given my own work a great moral boost. Of course, it goes without saying that the most vital help I received at the University came from our college secretaries: Annette Aragon, Micki Markowski, and Sharon Pruett.

ACKNOWLEDGMENTS

I would like to express great appreciation to the staff of the University of South Carolina Press for all of their patience and efforts.

I am greatly indebted to those of my colleagues who read a chapter of my final manuscript and provided valuable suggestions and insights: Margaret Barber, William Hochman, Doris Miller, and Cynthia Taylor. Special thanks to Will Wright, who looked at three chapters. More than anyone else, I would like to thank Bill Sheidley for his last-minute effort at the close of the academic year to read and comment upon my entire manuscript. He is a remarkable reader and an irreplaceable colleague.

Tim O'Brien once told me that he often goes too far in his efforts to please other people. After all he did for me while I worked on this book, I would have to agree with him. He let me disrupt his intense work schedule to interview him on two occasions. He also gave me six fascinating books to analyze.

Special thanks to Catherine E. Calloway for allowing me to cite material from her two remarkably helpful bibliographies.

Finally, I thank my wife, Anemone Schweizer-Kaplan, for her undying support. Her ideas and suggestions always brought me back to earth.

CHAPTER ONE

UNDERSTANDING
TIM O'BRIEN

Understanding Tim O'Brien

Career

Tim O'Brien was born in Austin, Minnesota, in 1946, and was strongly influenced by the conflict he encountered between the Midwestern environment in which he grew up and the decadence and violence of the world with which he came into contact when he left the Midwest. O'Brien was the first of his parents' three children. His father was an insurance salesman, and his mother was an elementary school teacher. When he was in the fourth grade, his family moved from Austin to Worthington, Minnesota, which had less than ten thousand inhabitants. According to O'Brien, growing up in a small town had a major impact on him. The same can be said of the main characters in all of his fiction to date, who come from small towns and are forced by often global events to see beyond the narrow perspective of the world they experienced while growing up.[1]

Storytelling and the imagination are major themes in Tim O'Brien's fiction, and his interest in these topics stems at least to some extent from the familial environment in which he grew up. One decisive influence O'Brien's father had on him was that his father was "a big book guy." He was on the library board and would constantly bring his son books to read. O'Brien's mother was an avid reader who would stay up all night to finish a novel, and there were always books strewn all over the O'Brien house. The family also spent a great deal of time discussing books and analyzing passages together, and they would talk about how scenes and events in a novel related to their own lives. "Books were around, talk of books, a love for books, love for writing."[2] O'Brien thus learned at an early age to consider stories and storytelling as integral parts of life, something that would later have a strong impact on his own work.

When he was eighteen, O'Brien enrolled at Macalester College in St. Paul, where he graduated in May of 1968 with a B.A. in political science. After he had completed college, his intent was to go to graduate school—either to become a professor and teach, probably political philosophy, or to get involved in politics, working somewhere like the State Department. His knowledge of political theory helped contribute to his growing criticism of the Vietnam War while he was at college, and during the early stages of the Vietnam War he became involved in the anti-war movement, "in the sense in which activism existed then." As he says: "From 1964 to 1968, while I attended Macalester College, there were no real demonstrations against the war. Four or five local activists might wave signs saying 'End the War.' I wasn't among those four or five people. I was, however, a big supporter of Gene McCarthy during the

CAREER

1967–68 period. I knocked on doors for him, took trips up to Wisconsin to help out during the primaries."[3] At Macalester, where he was student-body president, he wrote editorials against the war for the *Mac Weekly.* He had also read enough about the war to know that his own participation in it would be "ill conceived and morally suspect." Unfortunately, as O'Brien explains in his war memoir, *If I Die in a Combat Zone* (1973), when he received his draft notice the month after he graduated from college, the pressures he felt to fulfill his obligation to his family and country outweighed his misgivings about the war. Tim O'Brien was inducted into the United States Army in August of 1968.

Many of O'Brien's Vietnam experiences appear in his personal narrative, *If I Die in a Combat Zone,* and in fictional form in *Going After Cacciato* (1978), *The Things They Carried* (1990), and *In the Lake of the Woods* (1994). O'Brien spent his first seven months in Vietnam stationed about four or five miles from the American base in Chu Lai at a place called Landing Zone Gator. This is where he was officially stationed, but in *If I Die* he says that he spent most of his time out in the field, "walking around the area of operations in Pinkville—a bombed out, deserted, horrible place." One thing he does not mention in his war memoir is that he was wounded two months after he arrived in Vietnam. "Not a bad wound, but it hurt a lot and it scared the shit out of me. It was incredibly terrifying."

UNDERSTANDING TIM O'BRIEN

In all three of the books he has written based on his wartime experiences, he has confronted aspects of his past that were clearly painful to remember. However, according to O'Brien, he has never revealed some of his worst memories in his writings. He hints at the terrible things he witnessed in *Going After Cacciato* and *The Things They Carried* and candidly exposes his own fears and loss of self-respect in *If I Die in a Combat Zone.* Nevertheless, as O'Brien himself has admitted: "There are certain events I've never talked or written about. Things I saw or did in Vietnam that I've only told to a couple of people in the last four or five months. I don't avoid these events because people would condemn me—they would say these are things he had to do and he did them—but because people would look at me differently and I would feel differently around people, not because of who I am but because of the person I was."

O'Brien spent his last five months in Vietnam in the "rear," which is how he sarcastically describes a barbed-wire compound on top of a hill where he did a variety of things, such as pulling security duty and working as an adjutant battalion clerk. He left Vietnam in March of 1970, having reached the rank of sergeant. Of course, when one thinks of most of what O'Brien has written, it is difficult to imagine his having ever completely left the war. The way he once put it was that his "concerns as a human being and . . . as an artist have at some point intersected in Vietnam—

CAREER

not just in the physical place, but in the spiritual and moral terrain of Vietnam."[4] While he was in Vietnam, O'Brien began jotting down stories about the war, at least in part as a means of coping with the war. Gradually, these stories began to accumulate, and they ultimately developed into the war memoir he published a few years after the war. The Vietnam War also plays an important role in all of his novels. Had he not gone to Vietnam, Tim O'Brien might not have become a writer. As he once said: "I think I was kind of dragged into being a writer by life itself."

In September of 1970, O'Brien began studying government as a graduate student at Harvard University, where he remained enrolled for five years. At Harvard, he studied American foreign policy and began a dissertation that explored American military interventions. The background he obtained at Harvard on American military interventions was important to him when he wrote his second novel, *Going After Cacciato.* Equally influential were his readings in political theory: Plato, Aristotle, Aquinas, Locke, Dante, Machiavelli, and others. During this time he wrote his first three books, but he never finished his studies. Why? "That's what my mom and dad still ask. Partly because I knew I wasn't going to be a scholar. Writing was more suited to my temperament."

Like Stephen Crane and Ernest Hemingway, Tim O'Brien wrote his first novel while working as a journalist. He interrupted his studies at Harvard to work as an intern for the *Washington Post* in the summers of 1972 and 1973, and then he worked there full-time from May of 1974 until the summer of 1975. While he was at the *Post,* he was assigned to the national desk and covered a broad spectrum of topics, such as Senate hearings, veterans' affairs, the energy crisis. He even wrote some articles on the Watergate scandal. "Every day I wrote on something else. The lifestyle was torture, and I didn't like it much, although there was this thrill in being young and working for this high-powered newspaper during Watergate. There was also the terror of meeting deadlines, learning about a topic quickly."

O'Brien feels he learned several "writerly" lessons while he was at the *Post,* including how to work with active verbs and how important it is to obtain lucidity and clarity in one's writing. He also learned about stories. "There is a reason why they call them newspaper stories: You have to tell a story. I learned about organization, about what should go first, second, third and so on." All of this went into the broader context of his work as a writer, and his time as a newspaper reporter had an influence on his early development as an author. Working at the *Post* helped O'Brien improve his style, but it was his time in Vietnam that helped shape many of his themes and moral concerns.

Two other ingredients of writing O'Brien learned about as a journalist are discipline and tenacity. Writing dominates his life, and he organizes everything else around it. There is a line from Joseph Conrad that he likes to paraphrase: "Every day I go to my room religiously and sit down and write." After he refers to this line, he emphasizes the act of sitting down because that is how he organizes his own life—around sitting down at a desk and writing. "Everything else is peripheral to it. Books I may read, newspapers I may read, friends I may see, golf I may play. I make my decisions about when to do those other things around how the writing is going." Sometimes he will write for long hours, and sometimes it is only for five or six. "I used to be obsessed with it, to the point of being compulsive—to the point where it was no longer productive. But I have learned to wean myself away from the typewriter in recent years, and now I try to spend eight hours a day maximum, though I do treat it as a full time job. It's actually beyond a full time job because I'll work on weekends, on my birthday. In a way it is still compulsive, but it's not compulsive in a psychiatric sense—more in a writerly sense."

Like so many creative personalities, O'Brien lives much of his life in his head. In interviews he projects a warm and likable personality—his smile is often contagious—and he is deeply concerned about the world around him. He also goes out of his way to please other people, often, as he complains, to the point where it is no longer healthy or productive for him. Nevertheless, he always seems to be preoccupied with something that transcends daily life—with his stories.

Overview

Tim O'Brien is the author of the war memoir *If I Die in a Combat Zone, Box Me Up and Ship Me Home,* three novels—*Northern Lights* (1975), *Going After Cacciato,* for which he won the National Book Award, and *The Nuclear Age* (1985)—and two works of fiction that defy categorization, *The Things They Carried* and *In the Lake of the Woods.* All of his books deal in one form or another with the theme of courage, and he equates courage in all of his works with having the moral integrity and strength to take control of one's life and do what one knows is ethically right. His preoccupation with this theme can be traced back to his training in political theory and in particular to his Vietnam experience. Every book O'Brien has written to date depicts in some form a character's willingness or unwillingness to serve in the war, and each book also raises at least implicitly the question of which choice should be considered the more brave and decent. O'Brien believes that all great fiction explores moral quandaries and portrays characters who are confronted with making a difficult choice: "The reason choice seems to me important as a word and as a way for me to think about stories is that it involves values. It's most interesting when the choices involve things of equally compelling value."[5] A choice O'Brien struggles to understand in all of his works is his own decision to comply with his draft notice and serve in Vietnam.

If choice and courage are important words for O'Brien

in terms of the plot and structure of his stories, memory, imagination, and storytelling are three words that summarize his major concerns as a writer. As the following demonstrates, everything O'Brien has written since *Going After Cacciato,* up to and including a story that recently appeared in *Esquire* and his latest novel, *In the Lake of the Woods,* can be viewed as metafiction: as fiction that discusses the functions and effects of storytelling.[6] A main theme of his writings is that people create and live their lives with the help of memory and imagination. O'Brien does not just write stories: he believes that stories are a vital part of human existence. His notion of writing fiction echoes the critic Wolfgang Iser's revision of the antiquated opposition between fact and fiction in his recent study of the fictive and the imaginary: "Instead of harking back to the old fiction/reality dichotomy, I propose at the outset to conceive of the fictive as an operational mode of consciousness that makes inroads into existing versions of world. In this way, the fictive becomes an act of boundary-crossing which, nonetheless, keeps in view what has been overstepped."[7] O'Brien equates fiction and storytelling with exploration and discovery. In fiction the limited facts of memory and reality are reconstructed, and a boundary is crossed into a realm of infinite possibilities.

The process of exploring new possibilities by telling stories ultimately leads in O'Brien's works to a notion of reality that places storytelling truth above the veracity of facts. O'Brien believes that storytelling truth is often truer than the "truth." While speaking of the discrepancies between what might have really happened in Vietnam and what is told of the war in fiction, O'Brien said: "I think two hundred years, seven hundred years, a thousand years from now, when Vietnam is filled with condominiums . . . the experience of Vietnam—all the facts—will be gone. Who knows, a thousand years from now the facts will disappear—bit by bit—and all that we'll be left with are stories. To me, it doesn't really matter if they're true stories."[8] The truth about the Vietnam War is to a large extent embodied in the war's aimlessness, and this truth as far as O'Brien is concerned can best survive in stories.[9] Tim O'Brien edits reality in an attempt to dramatize important events and issues and lend them a type of clarity that they do not possess in the often mundane world of facts and literal truths. For O'Brien, a story is "true" when it makes "a believer out of your stomach."[10]

O'Brien's intense interest as a writer in memory and the imagination is reflected in the authors and thinkers he admires. When he was younger he was "obsessed" with the works of Hemingway and Faulkner, and the influence of these two writers can be felt in his early works—especially in the style and themes of *Northern Lights.* He also refers frequently to Joseph Conrad in conversations, and he strongly shares Conrad's fascination with the unknown. He believes John Fowles is "our best living writer," and he admires such authors as Graham Greene, John Updike, Walker Percy, Norman Mailer, and Tom McGuane.

Like many of the authors he respects, O'Brien is fascinated by the dichotomy between idealism and realism, and he values writers who deal equally well with portraying internal and external realities. Both positions "seem totally convincing to me intellectually, and this is reflected in the kinds of novels and stories I write, which take place not only in an objective reality—which on the one hand is totally believable—but on the other hand there is a character whose responses to it, to that reality, are almost entirely internal." All of O'Brien's stories take place both in the physical world and in the head, and both realms interact and modify each another. Also, in each book he has written since *If I Die in a Combat Zone,* he has contrasted realistic and idealistic characters. In *Going After Cacciato* he contrasts Paul Berlin, who lives in his head through most of the novel, with Doc Peret, who is a "realist" and insists on concentrating on the facts.[11] A similar distinction between the way pairs of characters think in O'Brien's fiction is made between Paul and Harvey in *Northern Lights* and between William and Sarah in *The Nuclear Age.* In *The Things They Carried* the idealist-realist conflict is embodied in the Tim O'Brien character, who is a sensitive and morally idealistic young man in the chapter, "On the Rainy River," and a revenge-seeking, realistic soldier in "The Ghost Soldiers."

Style

Tim O'Brien approaches writing novels as if he were working on a collection of short stories. When he initially began writing his first book, *If I Die in a Combat Zone,* he portrayed each incident individually in short vignettes that eventually became chapters. Later, he published some of these chapters separately before completing the book, and he thus established a pattern to which he has adhered ever since. O'Brien tries to make all of his chapters into independent stories, which have their own beginning, middle, and end. This approach to individual chapters reflects his concern with the tightness and compression of his writing. He also strives to give each of his chapters a sense of completeness because he wants them to possess what he calls their own "internal integrity."[12] Before O'Brien gets to the stage of actually writing a story, he first generally spends about eight months to a year trying to figure out the "moral aboutness" of his material and "how to dramatize it." That is, he plans a broad concept for each of his books, despite his emphasis while writing on individual stories.

Once O'Brien has reached the point where he is ready to sit down and begin writing, he spends his time concentrating on how to "make sentences and combinations of sentences that sound right and then work toward the creation of a dramatic dream. Rhythm is a big part of that. Dreams have rhythm. Drama has rhythm. The language mustn't be monotonous or repetitive."[13] One reason O'Brien spends so much of his time writing is that his style requires a great deal of revision. He usually puts a large amount of material down on paper and then works intensely at compressing what he has written. He compares himself in this sense to a poet: trying to squeeze things down and make his prose as economical and condensed as possible. In terms of his emphasis on efficiency, drama, and sentiment instead of sentimentality, O'Brien clearly owes a great deal to Hemingway.

Another essential characteristic of O'Brien's style is his tendency to make broad leaps between areas of internal perception and external reality: between the mind and the material world. On the one hand, like Hemingway's, his works are anchored firmly in nature: "Because life is anchored in these things. Another, more practical reason is that I have a hard time writing scenes that are set indoors. I feel liberated by a sense of space when I am writing; I like the sky, not a ceiling or a wall. Although conversation is a form of behavior, I would rather establish my characters less by what they say than by the way they behave, the things they do physically. And that means getting them out of chairs, out of the living rooms and sofas where too much stuff happens in novels."[14] The thinking in the second half of this quote echoes Hemingway's approach to characterization, in which showing becomes more important than telling. However, O'Brien differs from Hemingway and comes closer to Faulkner and Conrad in the way he often subtly moves from the outer world into the world of what his characters are envisioning or imagining.

Regardless of whether O'Brien is depicting the external or the internal world, a conspicuous stylistic device he uses to convey reality is the subtle repetition of words and phrases, as in the following passage from *Going After Cacciato*:

> Yes, they were in jungle now. Thick dripping jungle. Club moss fuzzing on bent branches, hard green bananas dangling from trees that canopied in lush sweeps of green, vaulted forest light in yellow-green and blue-green and olive-green and silver-green. It was jungle. Growth and decay and the smell of chlorophyll and jungle sounds and jungle depth. Soft, humming jungle. Everywhere greenery deep in greenery. Itching jungle, lost jungle. A botanist's madhouse, Doc said.[15]

The repetition of "and" links the mass of images portrayed here, and this device also helps convey the density and uniqueness of the jungle as Paul Berlin perceives it. He achieves the same effect by repeating the word "jungle" eight times and by emphasizing "green" throughout the passage. Moreover, O'Brien underscores the singularity of this experience for Paul Berlin with a stylistic device he frequently uses in all of his books: this paragraph contains only two complete sentences. Otherwise, he bombards his readers with sentence fragments containing images that become predominant because of the missing verbs.

The importance of repetition as a stylistic device in O'Brien's writings can be seen in the fact that he emphasized repetition and compression when he revised the text of *Going After Cacciato* for the 1989 Delta edition of the novel. In the original version of the text, first published in 1978, this passage is wordier, there is less repetition, and there are more declarative sentences:

> Yes, they were in jungle now. Thick, dripping jungle. Club moss fuzzing on bent branches, hard green bananas dangling from trees that canopied in lush sweeps of green, vaulted forest light in yellow-green and blue-green and olive-green and silver-green, algae multiplying in still waters. It was jungle. Growth and decay sweating green, the smell of chlorophyll, jungle sounds and jungle depth. It was true jungle. Soft, humming jungle. Everywhere, greenery deep in greenery, earth like sponge. Itching jungle, lost jungle. A botanist's madhouse, Doc said.[16]

The differences between the two versions might be minor, but they still point to O'Brien's increasing tendency to compress his sentences as much as possible. At times, his reductionist style almost becomes impressionistic, as in the following passage describing life in Paris in *Going After Cacciato*:

> They turned back to the hotel. Sunlight flowed through gauze curtains. He liked that. He liked the room's musty smell, a sparrow singing on the terrace, a vacuum cleaner purring down the hall. He liked it when she removed her gold hoop earrings.
>
> Details: the cool quiet he found in Place Dauphin on the Ile de la Cité, where there were pigeons and old-fashioned lampposts and chestnut trees. Someone practicing the piano in a salon across the square. A dog frisking in new grass. All the simple, shy things. A black man in a checkered shirt and purple pants playing *La Rose de la France* on his accordion.[17]

In an effort to depict a large picture with as few words as possible, O'Brien interweaves short declarative sentences with sentence fragments and piles image onto image. He also appeals to all of the senses without making a reader feel overwhelmed by sensory information because his style is suggestive rather than purely descriptive. The latter effect is achieved through the emphasis on fragmented images that lends the whole scene the feeling of a dream. The dream does not distort, however. On the contrary, O'Brien's style in this passage makes Paris more visible or tangible than a conventional description would. In this sense his style reflects his belief that fiction and the imagination paradoxically make reality clearer and easier to comprehend.

One thing O'Brien learned from Hemingway was to keep things simple. In his first novel, *Northern Lights,* in which Hemingway's influence is often too strongly felt, O'Brien at times uses simple sentences to the point where his style becomes dry or bland. This novel contains some effective prose, but it lacks the musical rhythms of *Cacciato.* The stylistic difference between O'Brien's first novel and his second rests primarily in the fact that in *Cacciato* he discovered how to use the repetition of words and simple phrases to lend weight and mystery to the things he wanted to convey. The repetition of minute facts and seemingly insignificant expressions gradually penetrates a reader's consciousness as the novel unfolds, so that they constantly gain in importance and vividness. In *Going After Cacciato* there are certain phrases that begin to haunt a reader, much the way a musical refrain sticks in one's mind. One explanation for O'Brien's habit of varying and echoing and repeating phrases and thoughts and scenes and stories in his writings is that this stylistic device mirrors his notion of fiction as a means for conveying the fluidity of all experience. According to O'Brien's approach to fiction, one can use the same phrase or tell the same story again and again, and yet each time one does so, the phrase or the story somehow takes on a new character. Fiction and language for him do not mirror life: they transform life.

Notes

1. Tim O'Brien discussed his life with me in an interview in Cambridge, Massachusetts, in July of 1992. Unless otherwise noted, all subsequent biographical information in this chapter, either paraphrased or quoted, stems from this interview.

2. Tim O'Brien, interview, in Ruth Bauerle, "On the Morality of Nuclear War," *Cleveland Plain Dealer* 27 Oct. 1985 (*NewsBank,* "Literature," 1985, 12:C5, microfiche).

3. Tim O'Brien, interview, in *Anything Can Happen: Interviews with Contemporary American Novelists,* ed. Tom LeClair and Larry McCaffery (Urbana: U of Illinois P, 1983) 264.

4. Tim O'Brien, interview, in Steven Kaplan, "An Interview with Tim O'Brien," *Missouri Review* 14.3 (1991): 101.

5. O'Brien, in Kaplan 108.

6. Tim O'Brien, "Loon Point," *Esquire* Jan. 1993: 90.

7. Wolfgang Iser, *The Fictive and the Imaginary: Charting Literary Anthropology* (Baltimore: Johns Hopkins UP, 1993) xiv.

8. Tim O'Brien, cited in Timothy J. Lomperis, *Reading the Wind: The Literature of the Vietnam War: An Interpretative Critique* (Durham: Duke UP, 1989) 54.

9. Elizabeth Mehren, "Short War Stories," rev. of *The Things They Carried,* by Tim O'Brien, *Los Angeles Times* 11 Mar. 1990 (*NewsBank,* "Literature," 1990, 4:B3, microfiche).

NOTES

10. Tom Dowling, "The Endless March of War," rev. of *The Things They Carried,* by Tim O'Brien, *San Francisco Examiner* 5 Apr. 1990 (*NewsBank,* "Literature," 1990, 5:B9, microfiche).

11. Tim O'Brien, *Going After Cacciato* (New York: Delta, 1989) 176.

12. O'Brien, in LeClair and McCaffery 268.

13. O'Brien, in LeClair and McCaffery 270.

14. O'Brien, in LeClair and McCaffery 276–77.

15. O'Brien, *Going After Cacciato* 28.

16. Tim O'Brien, *Going After Cacciato* (New York: Delacorte, 1978) 48.

17. Tim O'Brien, *Going After Cacciato* (New York: Delta, 1989) 263.

CHAPTER TWO

If I Die in a Combat Zone

Critics have referred to Tim O'Brien's first book, *If I Die in a Combat Zone, Box Me Up and Ship Me Home* (1973) as a novel, a collection of short stories, and as a war memoir. It has also been cited as an example of New Journalism in the tradition of Michael Herr's Vietnam book, *Dispatches.* However, none of these labels thoroughly captures the unique character of this book. Like all of O'Brien's writings, *If I Die in a Combat Zone* is not a book that can be easily classified. It is an autobiographical work, but one that reads like fiction, mainly because O'Brien uses so many elements from fiction in this book, such as dialogue, that one would not normally expect to find in a piece of nonfiction. He once described the process of writing *If I Die in a Combat Zone* as follows: "Often I couldn't remember the exact words people said, and yet to give it a dramatic intensity and immediacy, I'd make up dialogue that seemed true to the spirit of what was said. . . . I didn't follow the chronology of events; I switched events around for the purpose of drama."[1] It is precisely this effect of dramatic intensity that has caused so many critics to mistake *If I Die in a Combat Zone* for a work of fiction. Moreover, O'Brien's refusal to follow the kind of strict, realistic chronology characteristic of most war memoirs results at times in the creation of an atmosphere that

IF I DIE IN A COMBAT ZONE

resembles a fictional nightmare. The frequent shifts in discussions of time and place in the following study of O'Brien's first book are a reflection of the associative pattern of the book's structure.

O'Brien has called his war memoir a nonfiction personal narrative.[2] However, because he is mainly concerned with conveying the feel of the Vietnam War rather than mere facts about the war, O'Brien emphasizes in this book what the critic Eric Hayne calls the "factual adequacy" of his material rather than its "factual status"—that is, he seeks to convey the impact of the facts rather than their actual authenticity.[3] Like several other authors who wrote personal narratives on their Vietnam War experiences, such as Michael Herr and Philip Caputo, O'Brien adopts stylistic and narrative devices from fiction to make his readers *experience* the war. According to Hayden White's theory of the value of using fictional techniques in nonfiction, an author of nonfiction incorporates elements of fiction into his narrative "out of a desire to have real events display the coherence, integrity, fullness, and closure of an image of life that is and can only be imaginary."[4]

If I Die in a Combat Zone portrays Tim O'Brien's experiences and thoughts immediately before, during, and right after the year he spent in Vietnam. O'Brien allowed what he calls the "gravity" of his upbringing and background to draw him to Vietnam against everything he thought was right, and by succumbing to these external influences, he compromised his own individuality and beliefs. In writing this memoir, he attempts to purge himself of the influence of others by exposing and taking responsibility for his own actions during this critical period of his life. This book can thus also be seen as something more than just a war memoir. It is the candid *confession* of a young man who committed what for him constituted self-betrayal. Tim O'Brien submitted to outside pressures and fought in a war that he believed was wrong. *If I Die in a Combat Zone* is his attempt to confront and understand himself and his participation in the Vietnam War by *revealing* and *examining*—as opposed to explaining or excusing—the facts about this period of his life.

At the beginning of *If I Die,* O'Brien has already been in Vietnam for roughly six months, and the reader will later learn that almost a year has passed since the events portrayed in the second and third chapters—which trace his life before Vietnam—first occurred. The Tim O'Brien who appears on the first page is a seasoned combat soldier. He is no longer the average small-town American kid or the college intellectual O'Brien shows his readers in later chapters, but a cynical and mature soldier whom the war has numbed to the point where he has become indifferent toward all that is going on around him. The opening words, spoken by an infantryman named Barney, are, "It's incredible, it really is, isn't it."[5] For O'Brien, however, nothing is at this point in his life incredible. As he and the other members of his platoon make their way through the fields of Vietnam, being shot at sporadically has become a routine occurrence. The day O'Brien shows his readers in this opening chapter, "Days," is no different from yesterday. "Snipers yesterday, snipers today. What's the difference?" (1). The barren daily life in the small town in Minnesota where he grew up, the "Turkey Capital of the World" (13), has been replaced by a "vastly boring" existence in Vietnam.

O'Brien moves like a ghost through enemy country, and he responds to events with the indifference of a person who has lost the ability to feel. Moreover, this apathy of the foot soldier Tim O'Brien is echoed in the lethargic tone the narrator uses to describe the situation in which he finds himself: "The day was hot. The days were always hot, even the cool days, and we concentrated on the heat and the fatigue and the simple motion of the march. It went that way for hours. One leg, the next leg. Legs counted the days" (2–3). The combination of apathy and lethargy in such passages gives a reader the initial impression that the Tim O'Brien who appears in these opening pages is not completely alive. He lacks a firm identity, and he seems mentally detached from everything going on around him. Nevertheless, as the story of his Vietnam experiences unfolds, O'Brien gradually emerges as a fully developed and fully self-conscious individual. The Vietnam War thus becomes the physical backdrop for the portrayal of an individual's growth from someone who is acted upon to someone who acts and accepts responsibility for his actions. As a character in Robert Stone's novel *Dog Soldiers* puts it: "This [Vietnam] is the place where everybody finds out who they are."[6]

Despite his indifference toward the fighting going on around him, O'Brien in this first chapter still shows some concern for the other soldiers in his platoon. In the fifth chapter, "Under the Mountain," O'Brien claims that at the beginning of basic training "there could be no hope of finding friendship." He shuns what he calls the "herd," and he says that he "hated the trainees even more than the captors" (32–33). In all of the chapters portraying events that took place before the war, O'Brien feels nothing but contempt for the military and anyone associated with it. He sees himself as an intellectual, and all of the people in the military are boors.

Like the character he later created in his novel *Going After Cacciato*, Paul Berlin, O'Brien formulates his initial response to his fellow soldiers in an emphatic refusal to "join them."[7] Once he is in Vietnam, however, although he still hates the "captors," he comes to realize, again like Paul Berlin, that he is not so different from some of the other men around him. What he shares with them is not the kind of camaraderie under the pressures of war found in the John Wayne versions of battle. Instead, O'Brien discovers that some of those fighting alongside him believe as he does that "Horace's old do-or-die aphorism—'Dulce est pro patria mori'—was just an epitaph for the insane" (171). He explains that this was not because they were cowards, but because they were not committed, "not resigned to having to win a war" (170). When O'Brien first enters the army he feels alone in his hatred of the military and in his rejection of a war he believes is wrong. Once he is in Vietnam, he comes to realize that he and the Vietnamese people are not the only ones the American government and military are victimizing.

In the chapters where O'Brien discusses his life before the war, the pronoun "I" is dominant, but in the Vietnam chapters, the pronoun "we" becomes central, and it remains so until the last chapter where the "I" resurfaces. In the first chapter, for example, when O'Brien's platoon is hit with sniper fire, he views events from the perspective of the group: "We lay next to each other until the volley of fire stopped. We didn't bother to raise our rifles. We didn't know which way to shoot, and it was all over anyway" (1–2). Once he is in Vietnam, O'Brien no longer feels like he was singled out by fate to suffer alone, and he shows genuine concern and even affection for some of his fellow soldiers. O'Brien reveals this change in his attitude by shifting from the singular to the plural. Moreover, he underlines the importance of the group by repeating the pronoun "we" at the beginning of each sentence in this passage.

The soldiers the reader meets in chapter one, including O'Brien himself, are victims of a war that just seems to go on happening, without purpose. The title "Days" alludes to the policy of assigning soldiers to Vietnam for a limited number of days, 365, and not until the war was won or lost. Combat in Vietnam provided no sense of mission and no concrete accomplishments, such as winning territory, that could make it seem as if the days possessed some meaning. Instead, there was just the daily, mechanical routine of searching villages in the daytime and waiting for the mortar attacks to end before the night was over. "Things happened, things came to an end. There was no sense of developing drama" (7). For most of the soldiers who fought in Vietnam, there was not a clearly defined purpose behind the war. As a result, the war seemed like a sick and never-ending practical joke on those who were doing the actual fighting.

Writing about something as traumatic as war experiences can be taxing, but writing about a war that lacked a sense of developing drama presented difficulties with which writers of war fiction had previously not been confronted. As Philip Caputo complains in *A Rumor of War:* "Writing about this kind of warfare is not a simple task. Repeatedly, I have found myself wishing that I had been the veteran of a conventional war, with dramatic campaigns and historical battles."[8] O'Brien responded to this task by conveying the cold terror of his Vietnam experiences in a narrative tone that refuses to become emotional or interpretive.

Although the narrator seems thoroughly detached from the terrible situation in which he finds himself in the opening chapter of *If I Die,* this is not because he is apathetic toward the war and the devastation it is causing. On the contrary, once he is in Vietnam, O'Brien's opposition to the war and his distaste for those who are staging it are greater than ever. O'Brien uses a distant and often sarcastic tone to depict his wartime experiences, because game playing, sarcasm, and irony are among the most important weapons in *If I Die.* In "Days," for example, O'Brien and his two friends, Barney and Bates, joke about wearing the enemy down and causing the Viet Cong to use all of their ammunition. This scene reminds the reader of the American military's ludicrous policy of fighting a war of attrition in Vietnam.

In the fourth chapter, "Nights," O'Brien replaces the verbal irony of the first chapter with physical and mental games. The chapter opens with the word "Incoming," as O'Brien and members of his platoon dive into a foxhole during what seems to be a firefight: "As it turned out, the fire fight had not been a fire fight. The blond soldier and a few others had been bored. Bored all day. Bored that night. So they'd synchronized watches, set a time, agreed to toss hand grenades outside our perimeter at 2200 sharp, and when 2200 came, they did it, staging the battle. . . . Something to talk about in the morning" (25). In traditional war literature and in other works on the Vietnam War, it is not unusual to find soldiers playing games and practical jokes. Such antics are, in fact, part of the conventional camaraderie that appears in almost all war stories. However, O'Brien's portrayal of men at war more closely resembles unconventional war literature like *Catch 22* and *M.A.S.H.,* where humor and game playing are a principal means of survival.

The motives O'Brien attributes to the soldiers for staging the phony firefight seem thoroughly out of place in a narrative about war: they are bored and they need something to "talk about in the morning." Although one of O'Brien's friends calls their behavior nutty, O'Brien treats the incident as perfectly normal behavior in a war that made one feel like one was "in a cancer ward, no one ambitious to get on with the day, no one with obligations, no plans, nothing to hope for, no dreams for the daylight" (9). Before going to Vietnam, O'Brien was appalled at the prospect of fighting in a war that for him lacked a visible "cause" in which he could believe. Once he was in Vietnam, he seems to have discovered that one way of coping with the horror of fighting in such a war was to recognize that the whole thing was just a massive, macabre game. [9]

O'Brien also makes it clear at several points in his memoir that often the players themselves, the foot soldiers, determined the rules by which the game was to be played. In "Days," for example, while a lieutenant and a captain are conferring on whether their men should search some tunnels—one of the deadliest games played in Vietnam in the grotesque game of counting enemy bodies—the soldiers quickly destroy the tunnels by tossing several grenades into them and thus settle the matter on their own. In the chapter "Ambush," O'Brien introduces his readers to another game played in Vietnam that exposed the futility of the government's policy of waging a war based on body counts: "Often we had simply faked the whole thing, calling in the ambush coordinates to headquarters and then forgetting it" (84). A few chapters later, O'Brien shows his readers how these "phony" ambushes were executed, and he says that they were "good for morale, best game we played on LZ [landing zone] Minuteman" (103). The Vietnam War has been labeled America's living-room war.[10] It was a war fought against an elusive enemy for unclear reasons, while the American people sat back in the comfort of their own homes and watched the war being acted out every night on the six-o'clock news. It thus seems strangely appropriate that the soldiers who were in Vietnam also had an occasional opportunity to relax and watch phony ambushes, removed from physical danger.

Laughing at the absurdity of the war and seeing it as a sick game probably provided O'Brien with a means for surviving Vietnam. But Vietnam was still a war, and it was thus not always possible to just laugh at it until it went away. Sometimes it was just too terrible to escape. In the chapter with the peaceful sounding title "My Lai in May," for example, there is no humor and there are no games. There is only a scared and psychologically scarred young man named Tim O'Brien, "hollering, begging for an end to it," trapped in the middle of a never-ending battle, amidst mines and sniper fire and hostile civilians in every village (115). In "My Lai in May," O'Brien depicts a month of futile fighting against an invisible enemy and the searching of villages in one of the most "feared and special place[s] on the earth": the area the Americans called "Pinkville, a flat stretch of sandy red clay along the northern coast of South Vietnam" (113–14). At this point in the narrative, the war becomes threatening and very real.

In this chapter, more than anywhere else in the book, survival means staying alive by sustaining as much hatred as possible. Elsewhere, O'Brien aims all of his contempt and hatred at the military machine and at the political ignorance that gave birth to the Vietnam War. Here, however, the Vietnamese people and the land that feeds them are the targets. O'Brien makes no excuses for himself or others in this chapter as to why they at times felt such hatred toward the people and treated them so harshly. Philip Caputo, for example, tries to explain and possibly excuse his complicity in the evil of the war when he writes, after his platoon has demolished a village, that he felt at such times a "sensation of watching myself in a movie. One part of me was doing something while the other part watched from a distance, shocked by the things it saw, yet powerless to stop them from happening."[11] But O'Brien refuses to place such explanations between himself and some of the more terrible events in which he was a participant. "In the next few days it took little provocation for us to flick the flint of our Zippo lighters. Thatched roofs take the flame quickly, and on bad days the hamlets of Pinkville burned, taking our revenge in fire. It was good to see fire behind Alpha Company. It was good, just as pure hate is good" (117). This passage reveals what happened when it became impossible to keep enough distance from the war to remain sane. There is no irony here and no humor. O'Brien makes every word candidly reveal the evil of war. He does not apologize for the arbitrary brutality and destruction, and he does not seem concerned in this chapter with the rightness or wrongness of the war itself. He also does not view the events in this chapter with the intellectual distance of an outsider, as in earlier chapters. On the contrary, he openly admits that he too took pleasure in burning the villages and venting his anger and frustration.

In "My Lai in May," O'Brien expresses no indignation about the brutality of others that he witnessed:

When a booby-trapped artillery round blew two popular soldiers into a hedgerow, men put their fists into the faces of the nearest Vietnamese, two frightened women living in the guilty hamlet, and when the troops were through with them, they hacked off chunks of thick black hair. The men were crying while doing this. An officer used his pistol, hammering it against a prisoner's skull.

Scraps of our friends were dropped in plastic body bags. Jet fighters were called in. The hamlet was leveled, and napalm was used. I heard screams in the burning black rubble. I heard the enemy's AK-47 rifles crack out like impotent popguns against the jets. There were Viet Cong in that hamlet. And there were babies and children and people who just didn't give a damn in there, too. But Chip and Tom were on the way to Graves Registration in Chu Lai, and they were dead, and it was hard to be filled with pity. (117)[12]

In the first of these two paragraphs, two innocent women are subjected to a degrading beating, and an officer, the one person ultimately responsible for stopping such brutality, is an active participant in the war crimes. Moreover, in the second paragraph, O'Brien tells us in a perfunctory tone that napalm was dropped on these villagers, and the village itself was destroyed, purely out of revenge for the deaths of two American soldiers.

Such events are, of course, not unusual in the literature and films on the Vietnam War. In fact, it would be difficult to think of an account of the war in which similar scenes do not appear. What is unusual, however, is that O'Brien, who at least implicitly tries in this book and in his later works to "crusade against this war" (91), in no way tries to conceal his own participation in the "evil" that he describes. Instead, he chooses to indulge in such passages in what Paul

Fussell in *The Great War and Modern Memory* appropriately describes as "efficacious self-torment":

> Everyone who remembers a war firsthand knows that its images remain in the memory with special vividness. The very enormity of the proceedings, their absurd remove from the usages of the normal world, will guarantee that a structure of irony sufficient for ready narrative recall will be attached to them. . . . Subsequent guilt over acts of cowardice or cruelty is another agent of vivid memory: in recalling scenes and moments marking one's own fancied disgrace, one sets the scene with lucid clarity to give it a verisimilitude sufficient for an efficacious self-torment. Revisiting moments made vivid for these various reasons becomes a moral obligation.[13]

O'Brien says at the beginning of a passage in which he speaks of crusading against this war that after Vietnam he would also expose "the brutality and injustice and stupidity and arrogance of wars and men who fight in them" (90). He holds true to this pledge in *If I Die* by demonstrating in chapters such as "My Lai in May" to what extent war is a perversion of the natural order. A reader is shown in this war memoir how an extremely reluctant participant in the Vietnam War succumbed to the pressures of war and temporarily lost his humanity.

UNDERSTANDING TIM O'BRIEN

O'Brien's narrative strategy in *If I Die* is to take the stance of a reporter. He does not comment on the underlying meaning of events, and he does not take sides or pass judgment. In "My Lai in May," for example, the reader is shown soldiers doing terrible things after they see their friends being mutilated and killed by booby traps. However, O'Brien does not use these deaths to justify such actions. He also does not say that he acquired some valuable insight into the war or into himself as the result of such experiences. Things just happen in this text, in the same way things just happened in Vietnam, and the process of sense-making is left to the reader. "My Lai in May" thus ends like so many other chapters in this book—without comment and without a sense of conclusion: "Mail came. My girlfriend traveled in Europe, with her boyfriend. My mother and father were afraid for me, praying; my sister was in school, and my brother was playing basketball. The Viet Cong were nearby. They fired for ten seconds, and I got onto the radio, called for helicopters, popped smoke, and the medics carried three men to the choppers, and we went to another village" (119). In this one brief paragraph, O'Brien provides enough information for an entire chapter, but he conveys his material without commentary or emotion—as if nothing important had happened lately. Moreover, right before this closing paragraph, O'Brien says that he and his friends took a risky break from the horrors of the war and bathed and played wildly in the South China Sea.

Just before this scene, O'Brien's lieutenant, Mad Mark, is shown taking a potshot at a farmer in a field, whom he wounds in the leg. All of this is conveyed in a tone that suggests business as usual.

O'Brien seems to be convinced that what an individual experiences during an event as devastating as war cannot be classified under broad, general terms. O'Brien in *If I Die* is not merely kind or cruel, an intellectual or a soldier, but all these things at different times and to varying degrees. He might describe how he felt or reacted in given instances, but he never claims to have fully understood the meaning of his own actions or those of others while he was in Vietnam. Consequently he refuses to give definitive answers to the major questions he raises throughout his text, particularly to those questions concerning such ambiguous issues as what constitutes courage and cowardice.

One of the main values that O'Brien accepted as a youth growing up in a small town in the Midwest was that courage was not something to take lightly. Early in his life he learned that courage meant, above all else, demonstrating physical courage in defense of one's country. His induction notice, however, abruptly forced him to look at courage as a much broader issue. Suddenly, his country was calling on him to fight in a war he believed was wrong. From the third chapter, "Beginning," to the end of the book, courage for O'Brien primarily becomes a matter of acting upon what one believes is right, and that means summoning up the moral courage to say no to that which one believes is wrong.

The first test of O'Brien's moral courage comes in the third chapter when he contemplates ignoring his induction notice and running away. "I was persuaded then, and I remain persuaded now, that the war was wrong. And since it was wrong and since people were dying as a result of it, it was evil" (17). The question for O'Brien was how to act in light of such knowledge, and in the remaining pages of this chapter, he tries to answer this question. In "Beginning," O'Brien considers several possible ways of responding to his draft notice. His first thought is to run, based on his belief that the war was "wrongly conceived and poorly justified" (18), but his fear that he might be "mistaken" in his thinking forces him to reconsider this idea. His doubts about his own ability to determine whether the war can be justified are also compounded by his sense of obligation toward his country and toward the prairie: "For twenty-one years I'd lived under its laws, accepted its education, eaten its food, wasted and guzzled its water, slept well at night, driven across its highways, dirtied and breathed its air, wallowed in its luxuries. I'd played on its little league teams" (18). O'Brien equates fleeing from the draft here with something close to treason.

In order to avoid rejecting or betraying one form of authority—his country and the land that has fed him— O'Brien finds an answer to his problem in the actions of another authority: "I remembered Plato's *Crito,* when

Socrates, facing certain death—execution, not war—had the chance to escape. But he reminded himself that he had seventy years in which he could have left the country, if he were not satisfied or felt the agreements he'd made with it were unfair. He had not chosen Sparta or Crete, and, I reminded myself, I hadn't thought much about Canada until that summer" (18–19).

This sounds like a final statement on whether to run or fight, but this thinking too is later called into question in the chapter "Escape," in which O'Brien carefully develops plans to desert the army and go to Sweden by way of Canada. In essence, O'Brien's internal struggle over serving his country in Vietnam becomes emblematic of his greater struggle to come to terms with all the things he had previously accepted as established authority.

A key to understanding *If I Die in a Combat Zone* appears at the close of "Beginnings," where O'Brien again describes the forces that helped thrust him onto the battlefields of Vietnam. Here he refers to the dilemma with which he was confronted before going to the war as "an intellectual and physical stand-off" (22). He knew going was wrong, but he also felt not going meant abandoning everything he had previously known and accepted, which would lead to "inevitable chaos, censure, embarrassment, the end of everything that had happened in my life, the end of it all" (22). And so he went to the war still believing it was wrong.

To an extent, O'Brien compensates or pays for his lack of moral courage before the war by refusing, in this book,

to excuse his actions during the war. Like Joseph Conrad's
Lord Jim, O'Brien seems to be trying to purge himself of an
action that he conceives of as cowardly by bringing it into
the open and allowing others to pass judgment on him. Jim
gives in to the calls of others and abandons the passengers
of a sinking ship, and O'Brien surrenders to social pressure
and abandons his own beliefs. Both men try to come to
terms with what they feel is a cowardly act by struggling to
determine what constitutes true courage.

At the close of the chapter in which O'Brien contemplates desertion, "Escape," he has failed to execute his
carefully prepared escape plans, and he labels himself a
"coward" for this failure. "Escape" is followed by "Arrival," and for the next nine chapters the reader is exposed
to some of the horrors of being a combat soldier in Vietnam.
There are chapters on absurd military operations and practices, and there are booby traps and maimed bodies. One
finds humor and friendship alongside isolation and fear.
There are also atrocities and scenes of evil. But rarely does
courage become an issue. What matters in these chapters is
the reality of the war. Then, just at the point where it seems
as if thinking has been outweighed by action, by survival,
an entire chapter appears, one of the longest in the book, in
which O'Brien returns to his thoughts about courage.

In "Wise Endurance," while contemplating Socrates's
definition of courage in Plato's *Laches,* O'Brien continues
to grapple with the question of whether his going to

Vietnam was an act of courage or an act of cowardice. According to Socrates, courage is "a sort of endurance of the soul," but only "wise endurance" is truly courageous. O'Brien is thus also confronted with the question, "what, then, is wise endurance?" (134). He notes that having survived basic training, without "shivering in fear" like another recruit named Kline, was a form of endurance, as was getting through Advanced Infantry Training. He admits that he had almost deserted at one point and thus "almost not endured." He then asks himself if "the endurance, the final midnight walk over the tarred runway at Fort Lewis and up into the plane, was . . . wise." Or was his "apparent courage in enduring merely a well-disguised cowardice" because of his "failure to utter a dramatic and certain and courageous no to the war" (135). Finally, he wonders if it was wise endurance or courageous behavior when he watched "without protest" (136) while almost all of the men in his company opened fire on "Some boys who were herding cows in a free-fire zone. . . . I did not shoot, but I did endure" (135–36). O'Brien never answers the questions he poses in this chapter, but he also does not need to. He has already said toward the beginning of his book that he was a coward for going to Vietnam and fighting in a war he believed was wrong. His behavior thus falls under Socrates's category of "foolish endurance," and this kind of endurance, according to Socrates, is "to be regarded as evil and hurtful" (134). Again, O'Brien does not shy away from facing the consequences of his actions. He admits that he has committed an act that is "evil and hurtful."

After O'Brien has finished debating whether his own endurance could be called wise, he turns to some of his heroes in fiction and film and to the one brave man he met in Vietnam, Captain Johansen. He now tries to determine what it was that made these men brave. Here, too, he refers to Plato, who argues that courage "is one of the four parts of Virtue. It is there with temperance, justice, and wisdom, and all parts are necessary to make the sublime human being. In fact, Plato says, men without courage are men without temperance, justice, or wisdom, just as men without wisdom are not truly courageous. Men must know what they do is courageous, they must know it is right, and that kind of knowledge is wisdom and nothing else. Which is why I know so few brave men" (137).

O'Brien realizes he does not fall within this category, because he does not know or believe what he is doing is right. Still, he does know by the time he leaves Vietnam that he survived the war, that he was often scared, and that he belonged to the men who had at times sweated "beads of pearly fear, failing and whimpering," but nevertheless "trying again" (143). He comes to the conclusion in the last sentence of this chapter that maybe trying again and promising himself "to do better next time . . . by itself is a kind of courage" (143). This might not be wise endurance, but it is also not foolish endurance. It is not wise in that going to

Vietnam was not an action that displayed wisdom because O'Brien did not "know" it was right. Nevertheless, striving to be courageous in the midst of a wrong war is not foolish either. According to O'Brien, someone like Captain Johansen, who strove to be brave, "helped to mitigate and melt the silliness, showing the grace and poise a man can have under the worst of circumstances, a wrong war" (142).

O'Brien thus provides a definition of courage that he cannot apply to himself, and he admits that it is "sad when you learn you're not much of a hero" (142). Nevertheless, it is unlikely that readers of *If I Die* would in the end call O'Brien a coward, though by going to the war he allowed "fear" to keep him from acting "wisely." Ultimately he does display something resembling "wise endurance" by writing about the war and his own participation in it so candidly.

In the five chapters that follow "Wise Endurance," O'Brien returns to his portrayal of the war. Then in the second to the last chapter of *If I Die,* he suddenly turns again to the question of courage, and here too Socrates's authority is invoked. According to Socrates, courage is also the "preserving of the opinion produced by law through education about what—and what sort of thing—is terrible" (185). If one considers the fact that O'Brien could find the strength to write about the terrible aspects of the Vietnam War and in the process expose so many moments of his own fear, hatred, and cowardice without ever attempting to make excuses for himself, then one could argue that O'Brien does display at least a form of courage in *If I Die*: he endured what many consider the most terrible war in American history, and in his first book on the war he does a remarkable job of "preserving" what was terrible about it.

One of the "terrible" facts O'Brien exposes about the war in Vietnam is that the men who were forced to fight it were made constantly aware by the actions and decisions of their own leaders of just how futile and insane the entire endeavor was. He shows men at war risking their own lives and killing others for no apparent reason, men fighting in a vacuum devoid of all meaning. Probably the most striking example of this appears in the chapter "July." This chapter's title is indicative of the kind of understatement O'Brien uses throughout the book. "July" directs attention back to the only other chapter in the book that refers to a month in its title, "My Lai in May," recalling the scenes of senseless and cruel destruction depicted there. The title "July" also, however, can be seen as an allusion to the month in which Americans celebrate their own war of independence against an imperialist power. In O'Brien's "July," however, there is not much to celebrate.

The chapter opens with a change of command, as the brave Captain Johansen hands over his leadership of Alpha Company to a new commander, "a short, fat ROTC officer" who looks like a "grown-up Spanky of 'Our Gang'" named Smith (144). One of Smith's first assignments is to lead

Alpha Company back into the My Lai-My Khe area, a place O'Brien has already called one of the most "feared and special place(s) on the earth" (114). This mission begins, as so many others in the book, like a standard military operation, with the officers confident in their plans and objectives, and it ends in chaos and lunacy.

The plan was simple. Captain Smith's company was going to sweep through "Pinkville," accompanied by tracks, "armored personnel carriers, tank-like vehicles but without the cannon" (145), and flush out the enemy. Once the enemy had been forced out into the open by Smith's men, the tracks would simply gun the enemy soldiers down. By the end of the first day of this mission not much has happened. The men of Alpha Company have searched a village and found nothing more than a handful of peaceful villagers, whom Captain Smith decides to hold overnight as cover from a possible Viet Cong attack. Smith is proud of himself for having thought of the idea of using the Vietnamese in this way. He tells O'Brien, who is his radio man, that this was "Pretty good strategy" and that "ROTC's pretty good trainin', not so bad as they say. Hee, Hee" (146). In the next few pages it becomes apparent just how wrong Smith is about his own leadership abilities.

On the following day, the soldiers of Alpha Company sweep back through the same villages they had already searched the previous day, and Smith orders his men to search the bunkers and bomb shelters. No enemy soldiers are found, but a grenade "brought a lady out of her bomb shelter. She was seventy years old and bleeding all over. . . . Then we called in a dust-off helicopter, and when it arrived she crawled away on all fours, whimpering, trying to get back into her hole. The medics had to carry her. She hollered all the way. The bandages were dangling, blood was in her hair and eyes, she was screaming, but the bird roared and lifted and dipped its nose and flew away with her" (146–47). O'Brien closes this description of the first casualty of Captain Smith's command by stating in his characteristic noninterpretive and unemotional tone, "That was the end of the mission." Ironically, it is when the mission is over that the actual fighting begins.

As the men of Alpha Company are wading through a rice paddy on their retreat from Pinkville, up to their thighs in mud, they are attacked by the Viet Cong. The tracks respond immediately by opening fire on the enemy and rolling backwards across the paddy. "It was, we learned later, the standard maneuver when they take RPG fire, they go into reverse, full speed" (148). In the following minutes, chaos prevails, as the American tracks roll over the legs and bodies of those American soldiers who are too deep in mud to move out of the way quickly enough. When the fighting finally stops, the tracks have crushed several men. A soldier named McElhaney, who had vanished under a track, is finally found under two feet of water. "Most of the blood was out of him. He was little to begin with" (150). The men who have survived this chaos are standing around smoking when Captain Smith joins them: "He joked, he didn't smoke, he didn't help with McElhaney, and he asked what we thought about all this" (150).

Smith is an outsider, and not just because he is an officer. His failure to know that it was a standard maneuver for the tracks to move backwards when they were fired upon has resulted in several deaths. He nevertheless can crack jokes, which suggests that he is oblivious to the fact that those who have survived his first "mission" are probably terrified by the prospect that their lives are in his hands. Finally, he asks them what they think about "all this." When a weary O'Brien tells him "they should just turn the tracks around and get away from these villages," Smith disregards the caution and experience of a soldier who has been fighting in Vietnam longer than he and replies, "Well, Timmy boy, that's why I'm an officer. We've got our orders" (150). In saying this, Smith is echoing the entire chain of command and the leaders in Washington who were running the war: orders in Vietnam became more important than their consequences—the My Lai massacre was the most appalling example of this—just as winning the war became more important than any actual cause for which it was being fought. The "boys" who were doing the actual fighting and dying were ultimately only important as numbers that were measured against the number of human beings fighting and dying on the other side.

UNDERSTANDING TIM O'BRIEN

As Alpha Company moves on toward the next village, some members of the third platoon, whom Smith sends out onto a "broad, very large paddy dike," get blown to pieces by a land mine, "a huge thing" (151). The mine kills two Vietnamese scouts and wounds eight men, which brings the casualties in Smith's company to seventeen in a half hour. Smith, however, has something else to think about at the moment: "Captain Smith ambled over and sat down on the dike. 'Got me a little scratch from that mine. Here, take a look. Got myself a Purple Heart.' He showed me a hole in his shirt. It looked like a moth had done it, that small. 'My first big operation, and I get a Purple Heart. Gonna be a long year, Timmy. But wow, I've lost a lot of men today'" (151). There are few passages in *If I Die* that so perfectly convey O'Brien's remarkable restraint as a narrator of events in this book. If there was ever a place in the text where a reader would expect him to add a critical statement about what he portrays, then it is here. But O'Brien simply reports the facts and then moves on to the next set of facts, without comment and without emotion. O'Brien gives his readers the impression through his almost lifeless tone in such sections of the text that the war was so terrible that it would have been hard to express emotion or anger toward it without trivializing or compromising its portrayal. In this respect, the tone of O'Brien's narrative voice in *If I Die* echoes the tone found in so many important personal narratives on the war in which "one is always conscious of the authors' efforts to stay calm, to contain the shriek."[14]

Smith's behavior following the deaths of so many of his men—his preoccupation with his Purple Heart and his only being concerned with how his superiors will evaluate his first mission—can be seen as a parody of the egocentric behavior of the political and military leadership in Washington. Captain Smith is just the right kind of officer for a war in which body counts and "Peace with Honor" became more important than anything else—a war that was primarily an abstraction for those who were managing it. This becomes particularly evident in the scene that immediately follows Smith's showing O'Brien his wound:

> After the helicopters had gone, Captain Smith and the track commander argued again. We sat on the paddy dikes, the enemy presumably still around, while the two officers debated issues of honor and competence. Smith said the track commander should have informed him that they had a policy of backing up when taking incoming fire. "Damn it, I'm going to suffer for this," Smith said. "What's my commander to think? He's gonna see a damn casualty list a mile long, and it's only my first operation. My career is in real jeopardy now." And the track commander swore and said Smith should have known the rudiments of track warfare. He muttered something about ROTC. (152)

Smith refers to O'Brien throughout the opening pages of this chapter as "Timmy Boy," and Smith seems at first sight to be a friendly and jovial character. However, this passage makes it clear that he is a self-seeking and callous officer. He emphasizes what *he* has lost during this mission, the word "my" pops out at the reader as Smith speaks, but he is indifferent about the deaths his incompetence has caused. Like Lyndon Johnson and Richard Nixon after him, who were both afraid of being the first American president to lose a war, Smith is not concerned about the deaths that have resulted from his poor leadership. Instead, he is obsessed with what he might lose if the war does not run smoothly and according to his expectations. The men who have just died and the men who listen to the exchange between Smith and the track commander can thus be seen as the victims or pawns of a military machine that was oblivious to the destruction it was causing.

Captain Smith is intent on covering up or simply ignoring his own complicity in the evil of the war. The book's narrator, on the other hand, seems to perceive *his* mission as stating the facts about the war as candidly and objectively as possible, thereby exposing those things that were "terrible" about it. In the closing section of "July," for example, O'Brien provides his readers with some of the most brutal scenes imaginable of American soldiers in Vietnam being physically abandoned by their leaders, but he characteristically relates these stories without emotion and without commentary. In one of these scenes, O'Brien shows the aftermath of a five-minute firefight in which a platoon leader has been "mangled" and the "left testicle" has been "knocked off" a lieutenant (154). While all of this is occurring, a dustoff is requested for the wounded. A colonel, who has been "circling around in his helicopter directing things" and is nearest to the position of the wounded, replies that the men on the ground should "call into headquarters for a regular medevac chopper" (155). At the time, there is too much enemy activity on the ground for the colonel to risk his own safety by landing. Upon a second request for help, he replies: "Damn it, I haven't got time to do everything. Got to direct this operation" (155). Despite the callousness of the colonel's behavior, O'Brien passes up yet another opportunity to condemn those who were doing the condemning, and he simply proceeds to relate the facts about this mission.

In response to the colonel's refusal to help his own wounded men, the first-platoon radio man reiterates how urgent the situation is, saying that "his friend had a sucking chest wound and would die without quick help" (155). The colonel again refuses to land in the midst of a "hot" landing zone. He tells the radio operator to relay his "damn requests" through his commanding officer, Captain Smith. This gives the radio operator an idea, and he calls back saying his commanding officer is "unconscious and bleeding." Until now all of the pleas to save an enlisted man's life have been in vain, but when an officer's life is supposedly at stake, the colonel calls in jets to drop napalm on the village where the fighting has been taking place. All O'Brien says at the close of this scene is that once the village had been secured, the colonel "came down and picked up the wounded officer [the lieutenant who had lost his left testicle] and a dead man with a sucking chest wound" (155). The task of assigning blame for the soldier's death and of ridiculing the colonel's behavior is left to the reader. Moreover, by using the technique of showing rather than telling, which Hemingway employed in his fiction, O'Brien underlines his attempt to turn his memoir into a vicarious experience for his readers that rehearses his own process of growth.

O'Brien's style throughout this chapter, as in so many other sections of the book, is almost telegraphic: the sentences are generally short and precise, and adjectives and adverbs are noticeably missing. Captain Smith, for example, embodies everything that was wrong about the way the Vietnam War was fought, but the only negative statement O'Brien ever makes about him is that his "sense of direction was absurdly bad" (154), one of the great understatements of the entire book. Similarly, on the day following the incident involving the tracks, several of Smith's men are badly wounded and some others are killed by a mine. Since this time it is a mine that causes the damage and not enemy artillery, the battalion commander is suddenly generous enough to fly down and pick them up. O'Brien's only closing comment to this chapter is to tell his readers that the colonel "got the Distinguished Flying Cross" for his rescue effort, "an important medal for colonels" (156).

By refusing to pass judgment on the action in those chapters of *If I Die in a Combat Zone* depicting events that took place in Vietnam, O'Brien succeeds in portraying himself first of all as a character in his narrative. He is a foot soldier involved in doing what a foot soldier does during war: walk! "Forward with the left leg, plant the foot, lock the knee, arch the ankle. . . . Let the war rest there atop the left leg. . . . Packhorse for the soul. The left leg does it all" (26).[15] His legs and feet carry him through Vietnam, and he leaves Vietnam, unlike so many other soldiers in the book, with both of his legs, and his "legs make (him) more of a man" (125). O'Brien walks through the war, his left leg carrying his soul.[16] He also walks his readers through the war, showing them what it was like, but refusing to tell them what to make of it all. He informs his reader in the first chapter of his book that there "was no sense of developing drama" (7) in Vietnam, and he is true to this essential fact about the war by refusing to be dramatic about his experiences there.

The Vietnam War was a senseless war both militarily and politically, precisely because there was no viable justification for fighting it. It was a devastating war for those who fought it, at least in part because they were left without a sense of meaning or accomplishment as a result of their involvement in it. Accordingly, O'Brien resigns himself in this book to the inescapable fact that "the foot soldier [cannot] teach anything important about war, merely for having been there. . . . He can tell war stories" (23). O'Brien walks his readers through Vietnam in his stories, but he leaves it to his readers to find their own way back out of each story.

If I Die in a Combat Zone opens with Tim O'Brien walking through the mined fields of Vietnam, and throughout most of the book he continues to walk. In the chapter "Escape" he develops a neat plan for deserting the army, but in the end he tells us that he "could not run" (66). On the very next page he portrays his "Arrival" in Vietnam, and his first thought while looking at various parts of the countryside is that he might "walk to *that* spot and die" (67). During basic training, his friend Erik "enlists for an extra year to escape infantry duty," but O'Brien does not because he is confident that the army will use him "for more than a pair of legs" (49). However, he is wrong about this and, unlike the "terrified" recruit Kline, who is not shipped to Vietnam because he has two left feet, O'Brien ends up taking a "final midnight walk over the tarred runway at Fort Lewis and up into the plane" (135) to Vietnam.

O'Brien's walking his way through the war instead of running from it, as he planned to do in "Escape," anticipates his later action after the war of writing about his Vietnam

experience. Unlike many other writers on the war who tend
at least in part to place the blame for what happened to them
in Vietnam on their parental upbringing or on their social-
ization, in the end O'Brien takes full responsibility for his
actions both before and during the war. He has the courage
to walk his readers through his wartime experiences without ever attempting to justify or make excuses for what he
shows. In the chapter "Courage is a Certain Kind of
Preserving," the fanatical Major Callicles tells O'Brien that
courage is "The guts to stand up for what's right. Sure, it's
almost futile—like the last man walking around after the
bomb, just to show there's still people around, but it's still
something to be proud of" (194). Before he went to Vietnam, O'Brien did not have the guts to stand up for what's
right, but after the war he does have the "guts" to walk his
readers through the bombed and scarred mental and physical terrain of Vietnam and show them the terrible event in
which he was a participant.

In the title of the last chapter of the book, "Don't I
Know You," O'Brien asks himself something that he was
incapable of answering affirmatively before he went to
Vietnam. This entire book can be seen as his attempt to
explore his actions and experiences during this period of his
life in an attempt to uncover an honest answer to this
question regarding his own self-knowledge. Using a metaphor of a great walk or a journey, he gradually makes his
way through the rough terrain of exposing who he really

was before, during, and immediately after Vietnam. His answer in the end is simply that he is no one other than the person who has done and experienced all of the things portrayed so candidly in this book. There are no great revelations at the close of *If I Die,* and there are also no profound moral or political messages, like those found at the close of so many other books on the war. Instead, there is only O'Brien's highly suggestive observation in the last sentence of the book, just when he is about to land in his home state, that it's "impossible to go home barefoot" (203).

At the end of *A Rumor of War,* Philip Caputo confesses that the only atonement he could provide for his "sins" in Vietnam was that he had and would "endure."[17] Caputo resigns himself to the fact that he, and others like him, had "survived, and that was our only victory."[18] Similarly, the only thing a reader is told at the end of *If I Die in a Combat Zone* is that Tim O'Brien had endured, if not always wisely, the most momentous period of his life; and he had learned, among a few other scraps of truth, that the old men who sat in front of the courthouse of his hometown and told their war stories "had lives of their own and that they valued them enough to try not to lose them; anyone can die in a war if he tries" (202). Tim O'Brien neither ran nor hid from the war in Vietnam. Instead, he became a foot soldier and walked his way from being someone who had "compromised one principle" to becoming an individual who had

IF I DIE IN A COMBAT ZONE

"fulfilled another" (202). He had endured, and he had survived. He had also paid his dues to society, at the expense of compromising his own beliefs. In *If I Die in a Combat Zone* he honestly depicts and thereby at least partially atones for the moral and physical journey he made during this period of his life. In this sense, too, he did not go home "barefoot."

Notes

1. Tim O'Brien, interview, in Eric James Schroeder, "Two Interviews: Talks with Tim O'Brien and Robert Stone," *Modern Fiction Studies* 33 (Summer 1987): 136.

2. O'Brien, in Schroeder 135.

3. Eric Hayne, "The Value of Narrativity in the Representation of Reality," *Modern Fiction Studies* 33 (Fall 1987): 481.

4. Cited in Hayne 483.

5. Tim O'Brien, *If I Die in a Combat Zone, Box Me Up and Ship Me Home* (New York: Delta, 1989) 1. Subsequent references will be noted in parentheses.

6. Robert Stone, *Dog Soldiers* (Boston: Houghton, 1974) 56.

7. Tim O'Brien, *Going After Cacciato* (New York: Delta, 1989) 188. Subsequent references will be noted in parentheses.

8. Philip Caputo, *A Rumor of War* (New York: Holt, 1977) xiv.

9. O'Brien has consistently attacked the popular belief that the Vietnam War was somehow different from all other wars,

somehow more formless and thus crazier. As far as he is concerned, all wars are crazy from the perspective of those doing the actual fighting: "Every war seems formless to the men fighting it. Certainly if you read *The Red Badge of Courage* you get a strong sense that Henry Fleming doesn't know where he is at or where the lines are or where the enemy is. . . . We like to think our own war is special: especially horrible, especially insane, especially formless." Tim O'Brien, interview, in *Anything Can Happen: Interviews with Contemporary American Novelists,* ed. Tom LeClair and Larry McCaffery (Urbana: U of Illinois P, 1983) 267.

10. Compare Michael J. Arlen, *Living-Room War* (New York: Penguin, 1982) 6.

11. Caputo 306.

12. In one of the articles O'Brien wrote from the war for the *Minneapolis Star,* which is dated 4 July 1969, he describes a similar scene in which his friend Chip gets blown to bits and how "We took a POW after Chip died. I was a nice guy once, a real peace advocate—which I remain—a humanitarian. But I booted the dink around some, crying a little at the same time—crying and kicking, kicking that dink until maybe he'd turn into chip." Cited in James Woods, "Words of War," *Minneapolis Star and Tribune* 10 Mar. 1990 (*NewsBank,* "Literature," 1990, 5:B8–9, microfiche).

13. Paul Fussell, *The Great War and Modern Memory* (London: Oxford UP, 1975) 326–27.

14. C. D. B. Bryan, "Barely Suppressed Screams: Getting a Bead on Vietnam War Literature," *Harpers* June 1984: 71.

15. Within the context of O'Brien's use of a metaphor of a journey in *If I Die in a Combat Zone,* it should be noted that the book's title is taken from an army marching song.

16. Paul Diel says the "foot is a symbol of the soul, possibly because it serves as the support of the body in the sense of keeping man upright." Cited in J. E. Cirlot, *A Dictionary of Symbols* (New York: Philosophical Library, 1971) 111.

17. Caputo 315.

18. Caputo 320.

CHAPTER THREE

Northern Lights

In his first novel, *Northern Lights* (1975), Tim O'Brien depicts two brothers, Paul and Harvey Perry, who are involved in a desperate struggle to find some meaning in their lives. O'Brien takes many of the moral and existential issues that he raised in *If I Die in a Combat Zone* on the battlefields of Vietnam and places them in *Northern Lights* within the context of two brothers' battle with each other, with themselves, and with the past. In *If I Die,* O'Brien grapples with his guilt about succumbing to external pressures and fighting in the Vietnam War. As he examines his failure to display the moral courage to say no to the war, he becomes preoccupied with the question of what constitutes courage. Similarly, in *Northern Lights* Paul Perry has allowed the pressures of his upbringing and family background to keep him from living his life on his own terms. While trying to understand himself, his past, and his present life, again like O'Brien in *If I Die,* Paul Perry also strives to understand and summon the kind of courage it takes to seize control of one's life.

Paul Perry is the victim of an extremely authoritarian upbringing, and he feels imprisoned by the values his father has passed down to him. However, he does not come to terms with these values by attempting to reject or "overcome" what one critic, using Fromm's terminology, calls "his authoritarian conscience."[1] He simply reaches a point by the end of the novel where he can understand and integrate his two major conflicting desires: his need to be sensitive and introspective, and his desire to be brave and to act. Moreover, Paul Perry's struggle in *Northern Lights* goes beyond his need to deal with the authoritarian upbringing he received from his father. Ultimately what he needs to discover is that he has the moral and physical courage to confront all of the forms of tradition and authority from his past that have consistently kept him from saying yes to life in the present. As in all of his other works, O'Brien is concerned in this novel with questions of courage: with what constitutes courage and with what kind of courage it takes to do what one believes is right for oneself.

At the beginning of *Northern Lights,* Paul and Harvey Perry seem to have little in common, but as the novel unfolds it becomes clear that the values their father forced upon them during their childhood have affected both of them adversely. Both boys were taught that life is an almost apocalyptic struggle and that enduring it requires patience and, above all, what the father understood as masculine courage. As a youth, Paul generally resisted his father's attempts to make a "man" out of him. Since his childhood, however, he has remained tormented by the thought that he has never proven he could be a "man" in his father's sense of the word if he wanted to. Harvey, on the other hand, has adhered all of his life to the father's doctrine of "hardness" and endurance so tenaciously that he is in many ways a carbon copy of the dead father. Harvey has been influenced by his father's "masculine" values to such an extent that he has fought in Vietnam without hesitation, and apparently without remorse. Paul ultimately confronts his past, but Harvey never gets beyond trying to escape himself and his own history.

The novel opens with Paul Perry lying in bed. Like his brother Harvey, who is about to return from the war in Vietnam, he is "restless." He cannot fall asleep, and his fists are "clenching and closing like a pulse," an action that suggests his suppressed need to be fully alive and the monotony and aimlessness of his present existence.[2] In the opening paragraphs of the novel, O'Brien introduces his readers to those things that are keeping Paul awake. He is uncomfortable in the physical environment in northern Minnesota in which he was raised, with its incessant mosquitos. He cannot stop thinking of his dead father and of the bomb shelter his brother built for their father in response to one of the old man's last requests. He is tormented by his thoughts about the pond where his father forced him to learn to swim, and, perhaps most important of all, he keeps hearing a "sobbing sound," which the reader later learns is his memory of the sobbing he heard when his parents' third child died at birth. The death of the third child before it ever had a chance to live is symbolic of the two living brothers' inability to truly live their own lives.

Paul responds to the mosquitos and the "nightlong rush of images" that have kept him awake—as he listens "like a stranger to the sounds of his father's house"—by taking a black can of insecticide and "ejaculating sweet chemicals" into the forest and into his father's house in a symbolic effort to destroy the things that are troubling him (4). He is a person who is leading a boring and dissatisfying life, and he lacks any real identity of his own. It is thus fitting that he can ejaculate death but not life. Paul cannot create life because he is not fully alive. He can urinate on his wife's flowers (8), but the only form of sexual satisfaction he can experience is when she helps him masturbate.

Paul's inability fully to experience his wife, both physically and emotionally, is to a large extent caused by an aspect of his past with which he needs to come to terms. The Perry family history is marked by a conspicuous exclusion of all things feminine. Paul's grandfather raised Paul and Harvey's father, Pehr Lindstrom Peri, without the help of a wife. He also raised his son as if "he alone were responsible for its propagation, refusing to talk about the mother, ignoring the very fact of motherhood, an asexual northern temperament that excluded and eventually scorned things female" (69). The result of this upbringing is that Paul and Harvey's father ultimately came to the conclusion that "I

didn't have a mother . . . because I didn't need one."
Similarly, Paul and Harvey seem to have had little or no
relationship with their own mother, whom O'Brien men-
tions only occasionally, and then usually in connection
with the sobbing sound associated with the death of her
third child. In fact, the mother's name is not mentioned
anywhere in the text. Whereas the father's ghost still looms
heavily over his two sons, Paul and Harvey do not seem to
remember anything about their own mother.

Considering the male-dominated value system with
which the two boys were indoctrinated, it is not surprising
that both of them have difficulty maintaining a healthy
relationship with women. Harvey spends much of his time
and energy chasing after a woman who treats him like a
child and ultimately rejects him, and Paul's marriage is
incomplete because of his own confused attitude toward
women almost until the book's final pages. Just after the
scene where Paul vents his frustration about his life by
massacring some mosquitos—at a moment when he is
experiencing his typical confusion over whether it is better
to be "hard" like his father and his brother or to be "soft" and
give in to his wife's tenderness—O'Brien says that Paul
views his wife Grace as an alternative to the masculine
world of his father. However, he is still incapable of
deciding between the masculine and the feminine—between being tough and adventurous like his father and
Harvey or being sensitive and compassionate like his wife.

"He felt her studying him, that vast, womanly, wifely, motherly sympathy and understanding that both attracted him and repelled him, often at the same time" (12). Paul finds his large-breasted, mothering wife attractive, but simultaneously he is afraid of getting too close to her because of his enormous fear of appearing weak or needy. One of Paul's main dilemmas in the novel is that he wants to be soft, gentle, loving, and compassionate, but his memories of his father's emphasis on the masculine and his brother's constant challenges to Paul's masculinity and "hardness" will not allow him to accept this side of his character.

During the scene in which Grace helps Paul ejaculate, his thoughts shift back and forth between what his father and his wife represent for him. His thoughts of his father only remind him that, in terms of the father's creed of hardness and endurance, he is a failure: "Wings clipped by the old man. No bulls here. Rushing from nowhere to nowhere and learning to swim" (63). Paul's father and grandfather were preachers who both conveyed the same basic message: "simple heroism. What cannot be escaped must be endured, and if it must be endured it might as well be confronted" (71). For Paul, this message is embodied in his boyhood trauma of the time his father tried to teach him to swim by forcing him to go into the murky waters of Pliney's Pond near the family's house.[3] For Paul, this pond symbolizes the womb and life, but it also reminds him of his own sense of inadequacy. For the father, teaching Paul to swim in the pond was just one more way of teaching his son to confront and endure the things he feared. Even after his father has died and Paul has grown up and married, he still believes his childhood fear of the pond is indicative of his inability to confront and live life with the courage his father had always wanted him to display.

Whenever Paul thinks of how his father forced him to learn to swim in Pliney's Pond, he is filled with terror, but he is also somehow attracted to the pond because its soft waters remind him of the womb and of the sense of rebirth and life he so longs for. Paul's relationship to the pond, one of the book's most important symbols, thus mirrors his ambiguous feelings toward his own wife and father. The pond is soft, like Grace, who for him is "part of the pond, soft as water" (63). Also, like Grace, it is "fecund," fertile and full of life (9). However, the pond also represents one of Paul's first memories of his inability to please his father by being "bullish" and brave—the time he "waded bawling" into it. It thus symbolizes what he considers his two greatest weaknesses: his inadequate courage in the face of danger, and his inability to swim in the waters of the feminine.

Almost until the last pages of the novel, Paul is torn between the two poles described above: the hardness of his father and brother and the softness of Grace. Moreover, hardness in the novel is symbolic of the past and of tradition, particularly of the tradition of endurance and survival in the harsh climate and rugged life of the north. Softness, on the other hand, is symbolic of fertility, warmth, and a new life in the future. O'Brien equates being "hard" in this novel with living according to values handed down over generations, and it thus means resisting change. In this sense, being hard symbolizes leading a life that is stagnant, like the stagnant waters of Pliney's Pond, and like the stagnating, masculine values of the father that have led both brothers "nowhere."[4] Softness, on the other hand, has the potential to lead to birth and the renewal of life, again like the waters of the same pond that also contains "tiny capsules of cellulose, tiny larvae and mosquito eggs" (8), and like Paul's "soft" wife, Grace, who wants to have a child and whose name suggests redemption and thus the renewal of life.

The significance of Paul's struggle to decide between hardness and softness becomes apparent during the cross-country ski trip he takes with his brother through the wilderness of northern Minnesota.[5] During the first part of the trip, the hard and bullish Harvey leads his helpless brother into the unknown. O'Brien initially differentiates Harvey from Paul by the fact that Harvey possesses the kind of "endurance" and "vision" which the father so often praised in his fiery sermons. The reader is nevertheless reminded throughout the novel of the limitations of this "vision" by the fact that Harvey lost an eye in the "man's" world of Vietnam, and by the fact that he does not seem to have learned anything from his wartime experiences. Paul, on the other hand, who is thoroughly dependent on his glasses for seeing, and whose middle name is an allusion to the blind poet Milton, typifies the "blindness" and "softness" which the father scorned in his sermons. As he slavishly follows his brother through the woods, Paul is constantly reminded of the inner tension that has burdened him through much of his life: "It was that long far-back tension, a kind of tugging, a feeling of vast bewilderment and eventual melancholy at not seeing so clearly" (191). Paul's biggest problem, at least from his own perspective, is that he feels a need to free himself from the values his father and brother have tried to force upon him. Simultaneously, however, he believes he cannot do so until he can prove that he can live according to those very same values. The result is that his life is a standoff. He has never tried to "see" like his father and brother, and he feels an enormous amount of guilt and frustration over not having proven that he possesses their kind of vision.

Paul resembles Tim O'Brien in *If I Die in a Combat Zone,* in that he also does not fully accept all of the values forced upon him as he was growing up, but he still allows those values to affect his life. Moreover, both characters seem to believe that rejecting those values could result in censorship and social isolation, which they fear would be more unbearable than the guilt they feel over not making their own choices about the direction of their lives. Paul Perry in particular has been so incapable of deciding between the options with which he has been confronted in life—to follow the severe, northern "wind of his father" or the "southern calm of Grace, and all that it stood for" (191). As a result, until now he has simply allowed what O'Brien refers to in *If I Die* as the "gravity" of the past to determine his life for him. He has, in essence, based his life not on "choice," and even less on "pure inclination," but on "circumstance, genetic fix, history, events" (315). Paul is being pulled against his own wishes toward the north and the rugged and "hard" life it embodies by what O'Brien calls the magnet of the North Pole.

The North is the trap from which he cannot free himself, and in the North he is a victim of his own thoughts of being a failure. His father and his father's father endured in the north. They met its challenges head on, and Paul's brother has always tried to emulate them. For Paul, the north is thus a constant reminder that, unlike his brother, he has not lived up to expectations imposed upon him from the past. O'Brien refers to Paul throughout most of the novel as Perry, but unlike the adventurous Admiral Peary—whose name O'Brien spells "Perry" (174)—Paul is unable to live according to his family's golden rule: the big "A" as Harvey calls it, adventure.

The south, on the other hand, is not an exciting or adventurous place but a place that offers "shelter" and warmth, and the south is embodied in Grace, who is from a state to the south of Minnesota where toward the end of the novel she suggests the two of them might move. The south is also a place where life can flourish, a "stewing brewing simmering place of contentment" (192). It is thus symbolic of the future, at least of the future life that Paul, by the end of the novel, wants to begin to build for himself and his family on his own terms.

Before Paul can put his past in perspective, however, he first has to come to terms with it by seeing what his father and brother have seen. The chance for him to do just that comes on the cross-country ski trip he takes with Harvey. Early in the novel, the mayor of the town in which Paul grew up and still lives, Judd Hammer, warns him not to "let your old man shove you around. . . . Not Harvey either" (29). The father is of course already dead when Judd says this, but Judd's statement is quite accurate. Paul still is being shoved around by his father to the extent that he is still caught up in trying to be as "hard" as he believes his father was. Just after Judd expresses the above warning to Paul, for example, Paul equates happiness with getting into shape and reaching "bullhood" (31). Throughout most of the novel Paul is constantly competing with Harvey and trying to be as strong and masculine as Harvey. This all reaches a climax on the cross-country ski trip.

As the two brothers are about to depart on their ski trip, O'Brien suggests that this event can be seen as the culmination of all of the pressure Paul has felt during his life to prove he can be as much of a man as his father and brother. "The momentum of departure was taking hold, an inertia that seemed to have started years before, slowly growing until it was a locomotive that wailed down an incline, uncontrolled, and Perry held on, following Harvey's lead" (158). Paul Perry has spent most of his life either watching others act or following his brother's lead. He is, as Harvey's girlfriend Addie calls him, a "Peeping Paul." Characteristically, when his friend Herb Wolff tries to get him to sign up to fight a forest fire the townspeople expect to break out at any moment, Paul replies, "Not me, Herb. I'll watch it from the window" (49). And later in the novel, he has a dream that Addie is drowning, but instead of helping her, he simply watches (275), behavior that is in stark contrast with Harvey's, who heroically saves Paul from drowning at one point in the novel (78). He also watches television while his brother builds the bomb shelter for the father. Finally, years later at a local club, he watches the others dance. It is thus fitting that he spends the first part of the ski trip following his brother and watching Harvey's orange rucksack.

During the first few days of the ski trip, Paul is agitated and afraid he and his brother will get lost in the forest, which is exactly what happens. Then when Harvey's cough develops into pneumonia, Paul has no other choice but to take the lead and try to find some shelter. Precisely at the point where Paul begins to see differently and to realize he too can be "hard" and "bullish," he loses his glasses and is forced to find the way out of the northern woods without them.

The first sign of a major change in Paul's attitude toward the wilderness and the "hard" life comes almost immediately after Harvey has thrown a barrage of insults at him about his manhood. Unlike in an earlier scene where Paul allows Harvey's implicit questioning of his masculinity to intimidate him into trying to kill a rat in a junkyard, Paul now simply ignores Harvey's accusations that he is afraid.[6] He can do this because he is already in the process of proving Harvey wrong by successfully leading the two of them through and ultimately out of the wilderness.

At one point when the two of them stop to rest, Paul for the first time in the novel can suddenly appreciate the beauty of the rugged nature that surrounds him: "Perry sat and looked up the trail and tried to think it out. He was hungry but he felt all right. He admired the trees. They were green as summer, long and short needled spruce. Farther ahead, up the trail, they turned to birch but beyond they turned to pine again. All over, the snow sparkled. It was a fine bright day and he saw everything clearly" (237–38).

This passage is strongly reminiscent of a scene in Hemingway's *The Sun Also Rises* in which Jake Barnes has a similar epiphany while on a fishing trip in Spain. The use of understatement and simple descriptive words, especially in the last sentence, also suggests Hemingway's influence on this part of the novel.[7] However, unlike the male characters in so many of Hemingway's stories or novels, Paul Perry does not perceive his epiphany as a signal that he must follow the "man's" way of life to be complete. He realizes he now has something great to "remember" (239), and he knows he has been "absolutely and undeniably unafraid, fearless, simply acting" (240). Ultimately, however, he does not feel compelled to adopt Harvey's and his father's credo of endurance. On the contrary, after he has found shelter, warmth, and food for the two of them, he begins to think "about Grace, then about Pliney's Pond, then for a long long time about Grace" (262). Paul has proven he can meet all of the expectations imposed on him by his father, and his thoughts now turn to the feminine and, in terms of the novel's symbolism, to the future.

After the two brothers have returned safely from their ski trip, nothing really changes for Paul. He still appears to be caught in limbo in the dull and dissatisfying existence of his hometown, but after the trip, Paul nevertheless does begin to prepare at least internally for a change. Unlike Harvey, who leaps from one adventurous idea to the next but does nothing, Paul approaches changing his life gradually and cautiously. The first few months after Paul is home again, he keeps the beard he grew in the wilderness, probably as a symbol of his newly discovered manhood, and he does not replace his glasses. The fact that he suddenly believes he no longer needs his glasses does not necessarily mean his vision has been improved because he now better understands his father's form of seeing. O'Brien has already warned his readers early in the novel against taking the father's and brother's form of "seeing" too seriously. Harvey lost an eye in Vietnam, but as Judd Hammer tells us, "Losing one eye never hurt a blind man" (30). As if Paul suddenly realizes the truth of this statement, toward the end of the novel he goes out and buys new glasses, shaves his beard, and, just after he has dreamed of going to Pliney's Pond and finding the "start of things," he puts his father's house up for sale.[8]

The changes Paul undergoes in the novel's closing chapters are subtle, and to a large extent O'Brien never describes them in explicit terms. When Paul first leaves the great forest behind him after the ski trip, he has developed a strong appreciation and understanding of rugged nature. Civilization with its farms and fences now seems "somehow wilted and diseased" (302). Before he walks out of the forest, he picks up some snow and makes a snowball, "packing it hard in his hands, then he picked out a decent-sized evergreen and threw the snowball, missine the tree by a few inches, and the snowball sailed out of sight" (302). The fact that he misses the tree suggests that he will never really fit entirely into the world of "hardness" the way his father would have liked him to. Instead, toward the end of the novel, Grace gives Paul, who has proven he can survive in rugged nature, a tour of the finer, more intimate things in nature.

Paul and Harvey were lost in a forest of "millions of green pines" (301), but much of the forest Grace shows Paul, as "she noted, was neither pine nor birch, but rather soft tangles of weed and fern and moss and simple things. She showed him a delicate fern which she called maidenhair, plucking it from the soil" (335). In the novel's closing pages Paul follows Grace's lead in his daily life, which implies that from here on it will probably be her gentleness and not Harvey's "bullishness" that will help guide him through life. O'Brien also suggests just after Paul finds his way out of the forest that Paul is apparently better off with the side of nature Grace represents than with the side Harvey has tried to show him. When he talks to two woodsmen whom he meets in a restaurant where he stops to call Grace, they tell him that he was "Pretty dumb" for not having stayed in one place in the forest and building a large SOS fire that the airplanes could have spotted (306). This is O'Brien's second hint within just a few pages that Paul is not as cut out for the rugged life as he seems to believe he is after the ski trip. As Milton Bates so accurately observes: "To be sure, neither component of courage [the masculine or the feminine] is adequate by itself. Without the experience of masculine courage in the blizzard, Paul might never have come to feminine courage; he had to leave the womb before he could reenter it. When he does enter, it is not to become feminine himself but to assimilate the feminine dimension of a virtue already quickened in him."[9]

Throughout the novel, Harvey is perpetually torn between rejecting his father's creed and hiding behind it. Paul, on the other hand, does not reject his father's authoritarian voice, as Marie Nelson argues.[10] Instead, he integrates what he has learned in the woods about himself into his overall personality, so that he can take charge of his life at the end of the novel without losing sight of the importance of Grace and everything she represents. However, before Paul can feel like a complete person, one capable of both introspection and action, he must first confront and come to terms with his entire past as it is embodied in Pliney's Pond.

Northern Lights opens with Paul Perry restlessly pacing his bedroom in the middle of the night. In the novel's closing pages, he again appears swinging out of his bed, "his fists clenching and closing like a pulse" (342). At the beginning of the novel, he is restless because Harvey is coming home from the war, bringing with him all of the family's past pressures on Paul to prove his manhood. But toward the end of the novel, Paul to an extent has come to terms with his past. He has proven he can display the kind of vision and courage of which his father and brother always spoke. He has also taken charge of his life by selling his father's house in preparation for his break with the northern woods. Nevertheless, Paul has not yet completely come to terms with his father's continued influence on his life, and his confusion over how to deal with his past ultimately leads him back to Pliney's Pond—the beginning of it all.

When Paul goes to the pond at the beginning of the novel, he is wearing his glasses. Now he has forgotten his glasses and is forced to feel his way to the pond, "blundering" through the woods as O'Brien puts it. This scene recalls his struggle to find his way out of the northern woods without his glasses, only now he appears weak and without vision, much like he was before the ski trip. On his way to the pond, he does not notice the magnificent sky above him that has been penetrated by the sunrise and the northern lights: "A mosquito was trapped in his ear, dancing madly. He dug it out and another entered, buzzing in its frantic death dance, dancing madly, his father ringing in the death bucket, the hollow tinkle in Harvey's voice, the bells of Damascus Lutheran, the stone cold apse. He did not notice the northern lights" (343). Paul seems to have regressed here to the passive, fearful, and weak person he was at the beginning of the novel. He is again "sullen and hot." He is listening as opposed to doing, and again his fists are "clenching and closing." The fundamental difference is that this time he has come to the pond to confront it and all of the memories that accompany it.

As Paul inches his way into the pond, he relieves his bowels and thereby releases "the whole architecture of his northern world flowing sweetly to ruin in the hot waters" (344).[11] The pond has always symbolized both life and death for Paul. As he wades toward its center and comes closer and closer to immersing himself completely into its waters, he overcomes his fear of the pond and thus his fear of his past. O'Brien depicts Paul's second baptism in the pond as if he were describing a birth: "There was no wind. The waters were stagnant. There was nothing to carry him in one direction or another, and he floated dead still as a waiting embryo. In an infant's unborn dream, the future was neither certain nor even coming, not even the future, and the past was swimming like so many chemicals around him, his own black bile running like diarrhea into the pool of elements" (344). When he confronts his fear of the pond, Paul simultaneously returns to and faces what he constantly calls a possible beginning of things, and he can now make a fresh start. After he has drifted across the bottom of the womb-like pond, with its "motherwarmth," he emerges out of the water and sees "the great lights" (344). At this point, Paul's rebirth is complete. He no longer fears his father and the past, and he is no longer charging aimlessly like Harvey toward an uncertain future. He simply exists in the present, and is content with the recognition that life is "Not so bad, at all" (345).

For the first time in the novel, Paul is ready to begin living in the present and working toward the future. Instead of thinking about entering the pond, he has entered it; and instead of thinking of Grace's large-breasted, motherly warmth, he returns home and enters her as well, for the first time in the novel. As Paul is about to make love to Grace and help create their first child, he "smiled at an image of the old man, banishing it, and it was like the warm pond" (346). When his father's image appears before him in a similar situation earlier in the book, Paul feels forced to choose between his father and Grace. Here he simply smiles his father's image away. Instead of associating his father with the pond and the pond with failure, as he does in the earlier scene, he now turns to Grace as the life-giving force he has longed for. O'Brien closes his description of Paul and Grace's lovemaking with Grace's asking Paul if her breasts are too big for him. The fact that they are not is a final confirmation of his acceptance of the feminine and of life. Some of the ideas in this novel about Nordic attitudes toward life stem from Finnish mythology, and according to the Finnish saga known as *The Kalevala,* it was a woman, Ilmatar, who was responsible for the primary acts of creation.[12] It is thus fitting that after Paul has come to terms with his father's myth of endurance and bullishness, he begins to accept more fully the feminine role in the creation and continuance of life.

The closing pages of *Northern Lights* reveal O'Brien's characteristic refusal to present his readers with solutions to the moral and philosophical dilemmas he portrays. Paul Perry has neither accepted nor rejected the masculine values that were weighing him down at the beginning of the novel. He has simply learned to put them in their proper place and keep them balanced with the feminine values embodied in Grace. His father is no longer a threat, and Paul can accept that his father "*was* crazy. That was the terrible hell of it" (345). Harvey can also no longer make Paul feel inferior because Paul has proven himself to be more of a survivor than his brother, who he now realizes is doomed to escapism, which Paul thinks is "Too bad" (356).

By the end of the novel, Paul, who has spent much of his life thinking "pooor me" (14), no longer feels sorry for himself. If anything, he realizes that his father and brother are the ones who deserve his pity. Unlike them, he now knows how to assimilate the two competing forces that had until now been pulling him in opposite directions. Like Tim O'Brien in *If I Die in a Combat Zone,* he discovers that courage is something more than just "the charge." As O'Brien tells us in his first book, paraphrasing Plato, "courage . . . is one of the four parts of virtue. It is there with temperance, justice and wisdom."[13] And O'Brien concludes this line of thought with a statement about Hemingway's hero, Frederic Henry, which echoes Paul Perry's discovery in *Northern Lights*: "And Henry, like all my heroes, was not obsessed by courage; he knew it was only one part of virtue, that love and justice were other parts."[14] Paul Perry realizes by the end of *Northern Lights* that his father's and brother's notion of life as a process of rugged endurance is insufficient because it fails to include that which both brothers felt toward their father and toward each other but could never express: love.

Notes

1. In one of the very few critical discussions of Tim O'Brien's first novel, *Northern Lights,* Marie Nelson argues that O'Brien's first three books form a trilogy which traces its author's struggle to overcome his "authoritarian" conscience and learn to live according to the voice of his "humanistic" conscience. For Nelson, O'Brien's first book, *If I Die in a Combat Zone,* shows him grappling with his guilt over having succumbed to the "demands of an internalized voice of authority" rather than having listened to the "inner voice of his humanistic conscience." In his third book, *Going After Cacciato,* O'Brien explores what the consequences would have been if he had refused to follow the dictates of his authoritarian conscience by not fighting in Vietnam. And in *Northern Lights,* Nelson contends, O'Brien finally depicts a character, his protagonist Paul Milton Perry, who learns to understand and ultimately to reject the "conscience so strongly associated in our time with death, and to respond to the conscience that urges us to live—and to live with the fullest possible awareness of what it means to be human and alive." See Nelson, "Two Consciences: A Reading of Tim O'Brien's Vietnam Trilogy: *If I Die in a Combat Zone, Going After Cacciato,* and *Northern Lights,*" *Third Force Psychology and the Study of Literature,* ed. Bernard J. Paris (Rutherford, N.J.: Farleigh Dickinson UP, 1986) 262–63.

2. Tim O'Brien, *Northern Lights* (New York: Dell, 1975). Subsequent references will be noted in parentheses.

3. The name of this pond might stem from Pliny the Elder, author of *Historia naturalis*.

4. Towards the end of the novel, O'Brien summarizes the two brothers' dilemma: "Like twin oxen struggling in different directions against the same old yoke, they could not talk, for there was only the long history: the town, the place, the forest and the religion, partly a combination of human beings and events, partly a genetic fix, an alchemy of circumstance" (315).

5. O'Brien thinks the "wilderness stuff" constitutes one of the strengths of a book which otherwise in many ways embarrasses him, and most of the book's reviewers tend to agree with this assessment. See Martin Naparsteck, "An Interview with Tim O'Brien," *Contemporary Literature* 32.1 (1991): 2, and Bruce Allen, "Survival on the Slopes," *Newsday* 4 Jan. 1976 (*NewsBank,* "Literature," 1976, 2:B5, microfiche).

6. The scene from earlier in the novel about Paul's being afraid to kill a rat anticipates his later being able to provide food for himself and his sick brother by killing a muskrat in the woods. O'Brien told me in an interview that such parallels in this novel were consciously drawn. This use of parallels and symbols in order to suggest rather than to state a development or change in a character's personality is another stylistic trait of this text which is reminiscent of Hemingway.

7. In an interview, O'Brien admitted that when he wrote *Northern Lights* he was "strongly under two influences: one was Hemingway, one was Faulkner. . . . Unfortunately, there are so many echoes that are Hemingwayesque—language coming out

of Harvey's mouth and descriptions and things that get in the way." See Naparsteck 2.

    8. Throughout the novel, Paul associates the pond with the "start of things," which is why he must come to terms with it at the end of the novel before he can move on in his life.

    9. Milton Bates, "Tim O'Brien's Myth of Courage," *Modern Fiction Studies* 33 (Summer 1987): 268.

    10. Nelson 277.

    11. At a similar turning point in *Going After Cacciato* where the novel's protagonist, Paul Berlin, reevaluates his own ability to confront life, Berlin also walks into water to relieve himself. See Tim O'Brien, *Going After Cacciato* (New York: Delta, 1989) 57–58.

    12. For more information on this feature of Finnish mythology, see Juha Y. Pentikäinen, *Kalevala Mythology* (Bloomington: Indiana UP, 1989) 136.

    13. Tim O'Brien, *If I Die in a Combat Zone, Box Me Up and Ship Me Home* (New York: Delta, 1989) 137.

    14. O'Brien, *If I Die in a Combat Zone* 139.

CHAPTER FOUR

Going After Cacciato

When *Going After Cacciato* was first published in 1978, many reviewers called it the most innovative and most powerful work of fiction to emerge out of the Vietnam War. Some early reviewers praised the book almost exclusively as a war novel, and several subsequent critics have interpreted its unique style and structure as part of an attempt to find a way to portray a war that had no coherently delineated order.[1] Such an approach is unduly limited. As O'Brien has said, *Going After Cacciato* is "primarily a book about the impact of war on the imagination and the impact of the imagination on war."[2] This novel says as much about the interaction between memory, the imagination, and storytelling as it says about war. At least one early reviewer realized how far the book transcends its Vietnam War backdrop: "To call *Going After Cacciato* a novel about war is like calling *Moby Dick* a novel about whales."[3] Philip Beidler points out a main theme of *Cacciato* when he writes: "if imagination can in fact dictate the character of future experience, it must also be seen in many ways as having its own character dictated by the memory of experience past."[4] This novel reaches far beyond the war and explores how the imagination affects memory, how memory affects the imagination, and how people use both as indispensable instruments for getting through life.

GOING AFTER CACCIATO

The novel's protagonist, Paul Berlin, whose name alludes to a long-divided city, is a torn person when the reader is first introduced to him. He is torn between his yearning to be brave and the reality of his immense fear. He is also uncertain whether the right thing for him to do is to flee the war or to fight in it, and he has absolutely no idea of how to reconcile what he has already experienced in Vietnam with his upbringing and past. Like the others in his squad, he is just a kid, something that O'Brien emphasizes throughout the novel. But unlike most of the others, when the reader first meets Paul Berlin, it is hard to imagine him surviving the war. He is too confused, too fearful, and thus too vulnerable. Paul Berlin is a follower rather than a doer, which is symbolized in his being the last soldier in his squad and in his platoon in march formation.

In the chapter "Who They Were or Claimed to Be," the reader is shown a few of the poses or fictional personalities the other members of Paul Berlin's squad have assumed in Vietnam, presumably in an effort to stay alive. For example, Oscar Johnson—a black, middle-class buck sergeant from Maine—has used his imagination in Vietnam to create Oscar, the bad-assed shit-kicker from the streets of Detroit. Because of the behavior he develops to promote this image, he seems invulnerable to the dangers that surround him. *Going After Cacciato* is the story of how Paul Berlin also exercises the enormous power of his own imagination in an attempt to see himself as someone other than the scared young man the reader meets when the novel opens. Like Oscar Johnson, he uses his imagination to turn himself into someone who can survive the war.

Going After Cacciato contains three interlaced stories linked to each other through their emphasis on the Vietnam War experiences of the novel's protagonist and third-person center of consciousness, Specialist Fourth Class Paul Berlin. Sixteen of the novel's forty-six chapters depict the events and deaths Paul Berlin witnessed during his first six months in the war. O'Brien devotes another ten chapters to Paul Berlin's thoughts about these wartime events while he voluntarily stays awake through six uninterrupted hours of night guard duty in an observation post in Quang Ngai Province on the coast of the South China Sea. Since Paul Berlin is looking inward in all of the guard duty chapters, O'Brien symbolically labels them all "The Observation Post." In these chapters, the narrator also tells us how Paul Berlin creates in his imagination the story that fills the novel's remaining twenty chapters—the story of how Paul Berlin and the members of his squad pursue their fellow soldier Cacciato, who has left the war to walk to Paris.[5] The six months it takes them to do so, which parallel the six hours of Paul Berlin's guard duty, coincide with the six months Paul Berlin still has left in his tour of duty.[6]

About halfway through the novel, Paul Berlin attempts to formulate an explanation for his parents and the people in his hometown about why he and the others might have gone after Cacciato: "Partly it was mission, partly inertia, partly adventure, partly a way of tracing the possibilities. But it was even more than this. He couldn't put his finger on it, but he knew it had to do with a whole array of things seen and felt and learned on the way to Paris" (154). It can be argued that Paul Berlin does not just create the Cacciato story to get away from the war, to come to terms with his war memories, or to decide whether he should run from the war. Each of these things provides at least a partial motive for his strong determination to develop and complete his story. However, the main reason Paul Berlin pursues the story of going after Cacciato with such tenacity and fervor is that his imaginary journey to Paris is actually a very real and necessary journey into himself.

When Paul Berlin speaks in the above passage of the "whole array of things seen and felt and learned on the way to Paris," he is not referring to the sights he saw, to the excitement he felt over being in various countries along the way, or to the things he learned about these countries in the process. On his way to Paris, Paul Berlin sees how he has behaved in the past, and what he learns is how to behave differently in the future. A passage that reappears throughout the novel contains the parting advice of Paul Berlin's father: "You'll see some terrible stuff, sure, but try to look for the good things. Try to learn" (202). For Paul Berlin, who knows there are not many good things to be found in Vietnam, these words have generally meant using his imagination to escape temporarily from the war: "Curling inside himself, keeping an eye peeled for the good things. What would happen when the war ended. What he would do. How he would celebrate. Paris" (203). But as he starts to move deeper into the imaginary chase, he begins to discover that his journey to Paris is also a journey through his own memories and fears.

The character Doc Peret repeatedly advises Paul Berlin to deal with his fear by concentrating on the facts. Paul Berlin knows that if Billy Boy Watkins had followed this advice, he might not have died of fear on the field of battle. Instead, his fear probably would have been alleviated by Doc's very concrete observation of the fact that Billy Boy had a million-dollar wound—one that would have gotten him out of the war. Paul Berlin worries throughout most of the novel about not dying like Billy Boy, and he knows that one way to avoid a similar death is to overcome his fears. This is one of the main reasons he takes Doc's advice so seriously and tries so hard to concentrate on the facts when he tells his Cacciato story and when he recalls the war. He wants to confront in as much detail as possible his own enormous fear before it gets him killed.

Toward the middle of the novel, Paul Berlin recalls Doc's statement that "observation requires inward-looking, a study of the very machinery of observation—the mirrors and filters and wiring and circuits of the observing instrument" (184). As Paul Berlin *watches* himself pursuing Cacciato all the way to Paris he looks inward at his fears,

at his desire to desert, and at his more painful memories. A
result of his journey inward is that by the end of the novel
he has a much stronger understanding of himself and far
more control over his fear than he had before creating the
Cacciato story. In *Going After Cacciato* Tim O'Brien
provides us with a model of how writing fiction is an act of
exploration. As Paul Berlin chases Cacciato to Paris in his
imagination, he does what the Vietnam War poet Jack
Fuller says most writers do when they create: he learns
something new about himself.[7]

Paul Berlin would like to be the type of self-sufficient
and strong-willed individual generally associated with the
conquerors of the American frontier. This is probably why
his story about pursuing Cacciato contains imagery and
jargon from the classical Western film.[8] Like Oscar Johnson,
who creates a tough-guy personality and history for himself, Paul Berlin, as he creates his Cacciato story, begins to
see himself as someone who can survive the war. *Going
After Cacciato* falls neatly into the classical pattern of the
Western chase, with the posse going after the outlaw. The
Western imagery and terminology initially appear in the
first chapter, where Paul Berlin's squad is still pursuing
Cacciato. As his squad moves westward, Lieutenant Corson
tells them to "saddle up" (9), and a few pages later Doc
refers to the lieutenant as "cowboy" (14). But in the
imaginary Cacciato chapters, the Western imagery becomes much more predominant. Shortly into the story,

Stink Harris guns down a water buffalo, and afterwards he is "posed on one knee," like a buffalo hunter in a Remington painting (48). Stink then compares himself to a Western gunfighter with "Hands like bullwhips. . . . Fastest hands in the West" (48). Later when Berlin and his squad are in prison in Tehran, in "Outlawed on the Road to Paris," Stink also whittles a toy gun. "Like Dillinger, we'll bluff our way out" (203). Just after Stink Harris has killed the buffalo, O'Brien tells his readers that Paul Berlin "had the rare courage to peek" (48), which is one of the first signs of how his self-image is being affected by the Cacciato story. This is also the incident that enables Paul Berlin to meet Sarkin Aung Wan—the female companion who consistently encourages him to continue onward along the dusty westward trail.[9]

The morning after Stink has killed the one buffalo, Oscar puts a harness on the surviving buffalo—an important symbol of the American Western frontier. Then "Paul Berlin climbed up and took a seat next to the pretty young girl. He grinned. Oscar shook the reins, hollered gid'yap, and soon they were riding westward along the rolling plains [of Laos!] to Paris" (53). As Paul Berlin and his posse head westward, the reader repeatedly encounters this kind of language. There is talk of heading Cacciato "off at the pass" (66), or of hitting "the dusty trail" (83). When Paul Berlin drives the getaway car out of Tehran and into the Iranian countryside, it is "as in the steppes of the far Dakotas, wolf country" (219). Then, just after Paul Berlin has driven the car over the border into Turkey, and the goal of Paris is closer than ever, "to keep himself awake he did the old counting trick. He counted mesas. He counted flattopped hills with sides dropping like the walls of skyscrapers. Buttes and summits and ridges as in Old Mexico, ravines cut by sheer cliffs, caverns, gullies, and dried-up streams and land faults, lost sheep, and wild dogs, dividing stripes flowing down the center of the road, howls behind him, beats of the heart, Tatars hunting him on horseback through canyoned country" (220). The narrator could be describing a manhunt in the American Southwest here. When Paul Berlin and his squad drive through Turkey, the reader is told he now knew "the full meaning of desperado" (221). Cacciato and the men who chase him are outlaws in the eyes of the United States Army. However, as far as Paul Berlin is concerned, in this case, as in some Westerns, being an outlaw involves doing something that requires courage.

Despite the frequent intrusion of imagery and terminology from the Western, Paul Berlin never succumbs to the temptation of portraying himself in his story as a tough-guy Western hero. The courage he so longs to possess has nothing to do with the quick-draw courage of Stink Harris or the bad-guy type of courage of Oscar Johnson. Courage is a major issue for Paul Berlin, as he works out in his mind "how to behave" and whether to "flee or fight or seek accommodation" (73). However, for him it does not mean fearlessness, but "how to act wisely in spite of fear" (73). Clearly, Paul Berlin would have nothing against winning the Silver Star, but his main goal is to survive the war and "live a normal life, to live to an old age" (111). One of the things he wants is to find the courage in himself to do what is right. As he develops his story about going after Cacciato, he is exploring various forms of behavior of which he might be capable and trying to see himself as someone who can act wisely in spite of fear. As he creates his story and confronts himself and his own fear, he also gradually finds the strength and even the courage within himself to look at all of the experiences that terrified him so much during his first six months in the war.

On the first page of the novel, the reader is given the names of the men whose deaths Paul Berlin has witnessed, but the reader is not shown the grotesque ways in which these men died or the impact of their deaths on Paul Berlin until he is mentally prepared to look back on his wartime experiences and confront them. After Paul Berlin has spent about one hour at the observation post creating his story, he decides not to wake Doc Peret to replace him on guard duty. This is an action the reader would not expect from the Paul Berlin who appears in the wartime chapters. Paul Berlin decides to continue his watch so he can proceed with his story. He also feels his way in the black night to the ladder on the west wall of the tower and climbs down to the beach. By doing this, he exposes himself to a possible enemy assault. "It was his bravest moment" (58). Once he is on the beach, Paul Berlin then slowly and calmly walks into the sea and relieves himself. This brave action contrasts with the many times in the book when he wets his pants out of fear.

In the description of the above scene in the first edition of *Going After Cacciato,* the reader is told: "He felt brave. He felt good."[10] But in the 1989 revised version of the text, O'Brien also says why Paul Berlin now felt brave for the first time since his arrival in Vietnam: "He felt brave. Tonight anything was possible" (58). As Paul Berlin experiments in his imagination with the possibilities involved in going after Cacciato, he simultaneously begins to feel the excitement of seeing life as pure potentiality. He is also watching himself do something brave and wise because in his eyes joining Cacciato in his flight to Paris is an act of courage. Thus, although in the third "Observation Post" chapter he is completely exposed as he stands for twenty minutes in the South China Sea, he does not "move" and he is "not afraid" (58). This is a much stronger assessment of his feelings than in the earlier edition of the text, where O'Brien says only that he was "not moving and not thinking much" (84). Similarly, in the most recent edition of the text, Paul Berlin is not only "brave," as in the first edition, but he is also "gallant" (84). The reason his character has changed so radically during this one short hour of guard duty is that he now feels "in control. . . . Concentrating, figuring out the details, it helped plenty" (84). Paul Berlin is simply following his father's advice in these "Observation Post" chapters. He is looking for the good things and trying to learn something—in this case, about his ability to direct his own life.

Immediately following the above chapter, O'Brien depicts in chapter nine for the first time one of the deaths Paul Berlin witnessed, and this sets a pattern that O'Brien follows through the remainder of the novel. The farther Paul Berlin wanders in his mind toward Paris, the more capable he becomes of confronting his own fear and the incidents that have filled him with horror since his arrival in Vietnam. The closer he gets to Paris, the more he also confronts those experiences that have left the most damaging mark on his psyche. Moreover, episodes in the imaginary chase chapters are often based on incidents that occurred in the war, and things he imagines happening on the road to Paris frequently trigger a war memory in Paul Berlin's mind while he is on the road to Paris. Throughout the novel O'Brien emphasizes the fact that the imagination feeds on and transforms material stored in the memory.

A good example of how the imagination uses information from the memory appears in a scene just after Paul Berlin imagines meeting Sarkin Aung Wan. As she and Paul Berlin sit next to each other on a buffalo-drawn cart and talk for the first time, they are passing through the Laotian countryside, with its "Pink coral and ferric reds"

(55). These are the exact words used to describe the way Vietnam looked to Paul Berlin on the day he joined the war (225). Moreover, just after the parallel description of Laos, he talks about moving through the country on the cart at a buffalo's pace; and after the description of his first day in Vietnam, he recalls what it was like to move through the war at a foot soldier's pace. The buffalo cart is the weary foot soldier's dream-come-true.

Another example of the interaction between memory and the imagination can be found in chapter seven, where Sarkin Aung Wan's two aunts "moan" and "sob" and "wail" for their dead buffalo. Their mourning annoys Stink Harris, who killed the buffalo (55–56). The killing of the buffalo in the Cacciato story echoes the killing of a water buffalo in a war chapter (94), and later in one of Paul Berlin's wartime memories Stink Harris is shown pushing around old Vietnamese women who are annoying him with their moaning and sobbing (231). Similarly, the chapter in which Bernie Lynn gets killed closes with the machoistic buffalo killer, Stink Harris, being unable to deal with the blood and needles when Doc asks Stink to help him make Lynn's death more comfortable. Then in the opening of the next chapter, O'Brien shows Stink Harris "squirming to get away from Doc's iodine brush" (65) while Doc attempts to treat the bite wound Cacciato gave him the time Stink tried to capture him on the road to Paris. Furthermore, Bernie Lynn dies in chapter nine as the result of being shot in a tunnel, and chapter ten depicts how Paul Berlin and the others fall into a hole containing a vast network of tunnels. This chapter, "A Hole in the Road to Paris," is then followed by "Fire in the Hole," in which O'Brien shows another of the eight deaths Paul Berlin has witnessed. The latter chapter ends with Paul Berlin's company destroying a village out of frustration and anger, which is nothing more than a "hole" in the road by the time they are through with it (71). The tunnels at the bottom of the hole Paul Berlin and his squad fall into are one of many obstacles he envisions on the road to Paris, and each of these obstacles reminds him of a terrifying incident from the war—here he remembers his own participation in the total destruction of a peasant village.

Shortly after Paul Berlin and the others have recovered from their fall into a hole in the road to Paris, the sole inhabitant of the vast network of tunnels, Li Van Hgoc, invites Paul Berlin to look through his periscope. As on so many other occasions during the Cacciato story, the others are all sleeping, just as they are in the tower the night Paul Berlin creates his story. As Paul Berlin looks through the periscope, which can be considered a metaphor for his own imagination, he sees another of the deaths he witnessed in Vietnam. He also faces his own shameful behavior here as he recalls how he avoided the eyes of the other members of his squad while trying to escape being ordered to search a tunnel, the one in which Bernie Lynn and Frenchie Tucker get killed.

GOING AFTER CACCIATO

After Paul Berlin has finished using Li Van Hgoc's periscope to look back on the war, Li Van Hgoc tells him "things can be viewed from many angles. From down below, or from inside out, you often discover entirely new understandings" (84), which is precisely what Paul Berlin does throughout the novel. He uses his imagination to look at the things he fears and has feared from different angles to come to terms with his fear. O'Brien underlines the importance of this process in the opening words of the chapter that immediately follows the last of the imaginary tunnel chapters. In chapters thirteen and fifteen, Paul Berlin imagines having an opportunity to discuss the war with an enemy soldier, but in chapter sixteen O'Brien says for the second time that "They never saw the living enemy" (91). Another reason Paul Berlin becomes braver as he stands guard in the observation post is that in a sense he *has* seen the enemy, and he has imagined the possibility of an enemy soldier also experiencing the fears and thoughts of desertion with which he has lived.

A reason the war chapters do not follow chronological order is that in them the reader is given only that information which Paul Berlin is willing to remember or confront at a given point on his trek to Paris. After Berlin has imagined his conversations with Li Van Hgoc, for example, he recalls the month of July in greater detail than previously, and July was one of his worst months at the war. It was a time haunted by silence, the searching of tunnels, and unsuccessful attempts at driving the elusive enemy into "showing himself" (94). Had he not imagined his encounter with the living enemy, and had he not already looked back at the tunnel deaths of Frenchie Tucker and Bernie Lynn, he probably could not have confronted a period of the war in which the enemy and the tunnels were particularly haunting to him. This chapter on the quietest month of the war closes with Rudy Chassler breaking the silence by stepping on a mine. The next chapter opens with Paul Berlin and the others emerging out of the tunnels through a manhole into the hustle and bustle and noise of the streets of Mandalay. O'Brien structured *Going After Cacciato* like a game of Monopoly. Paul Berlin cannot pass "Go" and move on to the next phase of his journey until he has dealt with certain obstacles along the way, and these obstacles are usually his most fearful memories of the war.

At the close of the two chapters that take place in Mandalay, Paul Berlin tries to capture Cacciato, but some monks crush and beat him. Afterwards, his usual sense of fear turns into "Stink's kind of anger" (110). Then in the following "Observation Post" chapter, he decides not to wake Stink Harris so he can continue his Cacciato story. It is now three o'clock in the morning. "This was the dangerous time. He'd heard stories of how Ops were attacked: always during the darkest hours, whole squads blown away, men found days later without heads or arms" (111). The atmosphere here echoes the haunting silence of the chapter on July. Silence and darkness are things Paul Berlin has feared since his arrival in Vietnam. Instead of letting them bother him on this night, he continues to concentrate on the "million possibilities" of his story (112). The confidence with which he speaks of the million possibilities here and elsewhere in the novel stands in stark contrast to his thought on his first day at the war that there were "a million possibilities" of "places he might die" (41).

There is one major item from the past that Paul Berlin fails to confront completely—his own complicity in the murder of Lieutenant Sydney Martin. It could be argued that he struggles throughout the novel to recall all of the things he witnessed during his first six months in Vietnam, and tries to determine why and when they happened, primarily because he wants to figure out what caused this one horrible event to occur. Despite the importance of this memory for Paul Berlin, O'Brien never shows the fragging of Lieutenant Sidney Martin. Paul Berlin probably cannot fully confront what happened to Sidney Martin because of his own deep involvement in Martin's death. Had Paul Berlin bluntly told the others that Cacciato had refused to touch the grenade, and had he joined Cacciato in opposing the fragging, they might have backed off. After all, Oscar Johnson had told Paul Berlin that "Everybody has to touch it [the grenade]" (219). This fragging alone provided Paul Berlin with an ample reason for leaving the war in his imagination in an attempt to put his wartime experiences into a coherent order. Similarly, Cacciato showed courage in refusing to condone the fragging of Sidney Martin, but he too must have viewed himself as an accessory to the crime because he failed to warn Martin, which is also at least implicitly why he decides to leave the war at the time he does, shortly after the fragging.

When Martin's replacement, Lieutenant Corson, decides in a chase chapter to stop pursuing Cacciato, Doc and Paul Berlin try to convince the lieutenant they need him for the mission, to which he sarcastically responds, "You need me? The way you needed Sidney Martin?" (156). Then, just after Lieutenant Corson refers to Sidney Martin, the squad kidnaps Corson and they carry him onto a train headed for Afghanistan. (These are of course the same men who had killed Corson's predecessor.) Probably to run from the thoughts of Sidney Martin awakened by Lieutenant Corson's comment, Paul Berlin imagines himself riding away from Delhi on a "newer, faster train" (159). His mind also accelerates his movement away from the war, as he repeats the phrase "Flee, fly, flew, fled" (158–59). The train takes him into the mountains, but these mountains remind him of Lake Country in Vietnam where they murdered Sidney. What happens in this chapter, "Flights of Imagination," is the same thing that happens nine chapters later in another chapter with this title.[11] When Paul Berlin tries to accelerate the speed of his journey toward Paris, his mind pulls him back to his memories of the murder of Sidney Martin. As a result, he is at times in "two spots at once" (219). As Paul

Berlin and the others get closer to Paris, his memories of the war increasingly infiltrate the imagination chapters. It's as if his recalling mind will not let his imagination complete the trip to Paris until he has gained at least some perspective on the fragging of Sidney Martin and on how this event shapes his own first six months in Vietnam.

In the first of the "Flights of Imagination" chapters, Paul Berlin recalls his immense fear during the only major battle of the war in which he participated. He remembers how his legs were twitching, just as they do in the first and last chapters—the only two chapters with the title "Going After Cacciato." He also recollects how Sidney Martin made them search all of the tunnels they found in Lake Country, and how "It was there, high in Lake Country, where Oscar Johnson began talking seriously about solutions" (160). This is followed by the refrain "Flee, fly, flown." For the next few paragraphs, Paul Berlin is back on the road to Paris. However, he is already discovering that he can flee the war in his imagination, but he cannot erase the consequences of his own actions by running from them in his mind.

"Flights of Imagination" is followed by a short "Observation Post" chapter, in which Paul Berlin provides a brief "history" of his life and his character. The person portrayed here does not strike one as an individual capable of desertion, let alone of involvement in a murder. He is a quiet, daydreaming middle-class kid from the Midwest, who goes to war at the age of twenty simply because his country expects him to. He is also the same twenty-year-old dreamer who in the next chapter, "Atrocities on the Road to Paris," develops the story of a twenty-year-old Iranian soldier whose Government executes him for the same crime Paul Berlin is committing in his imagination—going AWOL. Similarly, the imaginary Li Van Hgoc was exiled to a remote maze of tunnels for desertion, and his punishment resembles the one Paul Berlin fears for himself if he deserts: being censured and banished by the society in which he was raised.

As the Iranian soldier is about to be beheaded, and while Paul Berlin concentrates intensely on the details, a fly settles on the boy's nose. Paul Berlin sympathizes with him thoroughly in his attempt to rid himself of this disgrace. This incident reminds Paul Berlin of some details of his own moments of shame, such as when he wet his pants in times of stress, "a wet leaking feeling that smothered fear in shame" (168). Again, it is becoming harder for Paul Berlin to escape in his mind from the war. The entire second half of this chapter, one of the longest in the novel, consists of a debate in a bar between Doc Peret and an Iranian officer on all of the ideas about duty, desertion, mission, and purpose that have been flowing through Paul Berlin's mind since the beginning of the novel. This debate culminates in Doc Peret's response to the Iranian officer's statement that "*purpose* . . . keeps men at their posts to fight. Only

Purpose" (178). Doc refutes this thinking with an answer that anticipates Paul Berlin's response to Sarkin Aung Wan at the close of the novel about why he cannot desert: "Maybe purpose is part of it. But a bigger part is self-respect. And fear. . . . We stick it out because we're afraid of what'll happen to our reputations" (179). Just after this debate, Paul Berlin's thoughts turn briefly to his observation post, and he marvels at how young they all are, both those still living and those dead. He thinks of all of the dead except Billy Boy Watkins, but again imagination and memory converge, and the chapter closes with Doc telling what Paul Berlin considers the ultimate war story.

Before Doc begins the story of Billy Boy's death, Paul Berlin slips out of the bar in an almost frantic effort to avoid listening to a war story he has consistently refused to confront. On the next page, in an "Observation Post" chapter, he then asks himself why so many ugly things are beginning to crop up on the road to Paris: "Why, out of all that might have happened, did it lead to a beheading in Tehran? Why not pretty things? Why not a smooth, orderly arc from war to peace. These were the questions, and the answers could only come from hard observation" (184). This passage is followed by the one quoted earlier, about looking inward and studying the "very machinery of observation . . . the observing instrument." O'Brien explicitly says here why Paul Berlin has to confront the ugly things—the war, along with the pretty—the flight from the war. The two are interwoven because both are part of Paul Berlin, the observing machine, powered by his imagination and memories. Paul Berlin cannot decide whether he can desert, let alone move toward alternate future forms of behavior, until he comes to terms with who he is and what he has done and seen. For this reason, as Paul Berlin again struggles to get the facts and the order of events straight, he picks up the starlight scope and begins to concentrate on the night. Like Li Van Hgoc's periscope, which helps Paul see things from different angles, this starlight scope can be seen as a symbol of Paul Berlin the observing machine. As he concentrates on the night and on the order of things, he finally finds the strength to remember in detail "how on the first day of the war he had witnessed the ultimate war story" (185).

After Paul Berlin has recalled his first day at the war and the death of Billy Boy, he returns in his imagination to Tehran, where they have all been arrested for the second time and are awaiting execution. Interestingly enough, Paul Berlin does not seem to be afraid in the two prison chapters that follow. He has confronted Billy Boy's death, and he is more prepared than ever to figure out the facts: "Billy Boy Watkins, like the others, was among the dead. . . . It was a fact. It was the first fact, and leading from it were other facts. Now it was merely a matter of following the facts to where they ended" (196). The tone of this statement is much calmer than passages from earlier in the novel in which Paul Berlin recalls Billy Boy's death. As Paul Berlin confronts and examines each piece of his war experience from many angles, he gradually becomes more composed and more self-confident. Simultaneously, as he becomes calmer and more secure, he seems more willing than ever to confront the uglier "facts" of his wartime experiences. In chapter thirty-three, they are all trapped in Iran, a country with a corrupt dictatorship that the United States supported. Their own government has also refused to support them— it does not "know" them. And O'Brien labels their "mission" an "alibi to cover cowardice" (206). It sounds like they are back in the nightmare of Vietnam just before they kill Sidney Martin, which is exactly where Paul Berlin now takes them.

In the next few chapters, Paul Berlin goes as far as he will ever go in remembering Sidney Martin's death. Just before the chapters in which he recalls the fragging, he and the others are forced by their Iranian interrogator to confess that their "mission" is an "alibi to cover cowardice," and they admit that they are "clowns" and "stupid." It is hard not to believe, especially since this comes immediately before the two chapters describing the fragging of Sidney Martin, that these confessions also apply to Paul Berlin and the others for their act of murder. They kill Sidney Martin because they are all afraid one of them might be the next one he sends into a tunnel. Only Cacciato refuses to touch the grenade in the two chapters on the fragging, and it is thus not surprising that in Paul Berlin's mind it is also Cacciato who comes to the rescue when they are all awaiting execution in Tehran. Cacciato embodies the innocence Paul Berlin and the members of his squad have lost, and it is probably no coincidence that after he has become a reluctant accessory in the murder of Sidney Martin, he too gets lost.

Cacciato, the pursued, is the "guide" on the "expedition," as Paul Berlin perceives him, again borrowing terminology from the Western. In the 1989 revised edition of the novel, O'Brien adds a statement in the first chapter absent from the earlier edition that Cacciato was "Luring them on" (16). He is the "light of the world" (37), leading Paul Berlin farther and farther into himself, and closer and closer to a recognition of what he has experienced and how he has behaved in the war. Ironically, the "dummy" Cacciato is the only person in the novel who shows Paul Berlin what it means to display moral and physical courage. Moreover, he is much more like Paul Berlin than Berlin is willing to admit. Cacciato uses his imagination to cope with the war, such as when he escapes the horrors of Lake Country by *concentrating* on his fishing all day. O'Brien ironically juxtaposes these two characters. When Cacciato helps Paul Berlin and the others escape from jail, Cacciato "whispered" and then "shouted" the word "go," which is the same word Paul Berlin "whispered" and "shouted" when they attempt to capture Cacciato at the end of chapters one and forty-five (23, 215–16, 289). In Paul Berlin's mind, Cacciato is apparently as anxious to see Paul Berlin make it to Paris as Paul is about seeing Cacciato make it.

When Paul Berlin and the others escape from jail, Oscar drives the getaway car. Oscar often takes over in the novel, and each time he does, there is an implicit reference to the fragging of Sidney Martin he orchestrated in the World's Greatest Lake Country. In Paris, he harasses Paul Berlin about resuming the search for Cacciato because "If he wins, we lose" (278). Oscar uses the same logic to justify murdering Lieutenant Sidney Martin. Paul Berlin tries to convince Oscar in Paris that there are other options, such as turning themselves in at the American Embassy. This reminds one of Pederson and Cacciato suggesting alternatives to killing Sidney Martin, such as talking with the man. Oscar, however, responds in Paris as he does in the Lake Country: "The game, it ain't played by those rules" (277). Finally, at the end of the novel, when they are about to capture Cacciato in Paris, Oscar also has all of them touch Cacciato's M16 rifle, just as he requires that each of them touch the grenade they are going to use to kill Sidney Martin. As always in this novel and in life, memory provides imagination with its raw material.

Shortly after the escape from Tehran, Paul Berlin takes the wheel, and this, along with the fact that he has not shown any great fear while in prison in Tehran or during the escape, is a sign that he is taking increasingly more responsibility for and *control* of his life and memories. Thus, as

Paul Berlin drives the group of "refugees" toward Paris, he finally confronts his own very deep complicity in the death of Sidney Martin:

> He remembered it. "Everybody has to touch it," was what Oscar Johnson had said. "He'll listen to you. Go talk to him." So, sure, he'd gone down to the crater to talk sense to the kid. "Hopeless," he'd said. "And it's for your own damn good, and even if you don't join in, even so, it'll happen anyway, but, look, it's for your own good." So he'd pressed the grenade against Cacciato's limp hand. Was it touching? Was it volition? Maybe so, maybe not. "That's everybody," Oscar said afterward.
>
> "A sad thing," Cacciato had said the day afterward.
>
> A very sad thing. Cacciato was dumb, but he was right. What happened to Lieutenant Sidney Martin was a very sad thing.
>
> Paul Berlin squeezed the wheel and hung on. (219–20)

Berlin has remembered the above scene on two other occasions, but he has never admitted to himself so openly that he possibly could have stopped the fragging if he had wanted to. The reference to Cacciato's "limp hand" gives the reader the impression that Paul Berlin already knows the answer to the questions he asks in the above passage about Cacciato's attitude toward the fragging. If Paul Berlin had shown the courage to accept Cacciato's judgment of the fragging and joined him in saying no, the young officer who had admired Paul Berlin as he marched in the chapter "The Way It Mostly Was" might not have been murdered.

The characters accompanying Paul Berlin on the road to Paris are the only surviving or remaining members of his squad who were involved in the murder of Sidney Martin, and it was only a small group out of over thirty men in Martin's whole platoon who were responsible for his death. Pederson only very reluctantly supported the fragging, and he has since been killed. Vaught and Ben Nystrom have both left the war because of self-inflicted wounds. Harold Murphy is the only surviving member of the squad who was with them at the time of the fragging, but in Paul Berlin's story, Murphy refuses to join them in their pursuit of Cacciato. At the beginning of "Lake Country," Harold Murphy also looks away from Oscar when the latter smiles at him over the idea of killing Sidney Martin. This suggests that he too might have been only a reluctant participant. This is possibly why he chooses to turn back in Paul Berlin's imaginary journey, rather than continue on to Paris with the others.

During each phase of the imaginary journey, Paul Berlin confronts some major events that led up to the fragging. At the beginning of the Cacciato story, the mood is generally lighthearted and adventurous, but as Paul

Berlin gradually develops his "idea," things become more serious in tone. By the close of chapter seven, for example, O'Brien refers to a trail of M&Ms that Cacciato has left behind on the road to Paris. This is followed by a brief "Observation Post" chapter. Then comes a description of how Sidney Martin sent Bernie Lynn to his death, which begins with the words "Get me the M&Ms" (59). Right after Bernie Lynn gets shot through the throat in a tunnel, Paul Berlin and the others fall into a hole on the road to Paris containing an ominous network of tunnels. They do not escape from the tunnels until Paul Berlin has confronted the tunnel deaths of Bernie Lynn and Frenchie Tucker, both of which are later used by Oscar to justify the fragging of Sidney Martin. In fact, at the end of the chapter immediately preceding the one in which Paul Berlin and the others emerge out of the hole into the streets of Mandalay, Sidney Martin looks directly at Oscar and says: "If tunnels were found [in the village they are about to enter] they would be searched" (96).

O'Brien follows a similar pattern throughout the novel, and it must be emphasized that when Paul Berlin speaks toward the novel's close of the limits of the imagination, he is speaking of this very pattern. His imagination allows him to explore the possibilities of running from the war, but it will not and cannot enable him to escape the consequences of running. Similarly, his imagination has helped him at times to escape the war and the things he has witnessed and done, but the consequences of his actions and those of the others cannot be erased by the imagination. Sidney Martin, for example, is dead. People can use their imaginations to view things from the past from different angles, and the imagination can change them and make them less harmful to the psyche. The imagination can also be used to come to a better understanding of past events. However, the imagination cannot destroy the reality of past events, because people need what they know to imagine alternatives. This is why Paul Berlin's imaginary journey to Paris is interrupted at various points by obstacles that will not let him continue until he remembers certain things, the most important "things seen and felt and learned on the road to Paris."

After Paul Berlin and the others emerge from the hole in the road to Paris, they experience some good times in Mandalay and later in Delhi. At a restaurant in Mandalay, they relax, have a good meal, and toast to "peace and domestic tranquility.... To all the memories, may they rest in peace" (106). But the memories refuse to rest. Sure, as they settle down in Delhi for a brief period, Paul Berlin can imagine a period of "asylum" and "repose" on the way to Paris. However, shortly after this, they become trapped in Tehran and are not able to resume their journey until Paul Berlin has finally confronted the death of Billy Boy Watkins and begun to think about the murder of Sidney Martin.

As Berlin speeds through Turkey on his way to the sea, he has his last and most candid thoughts about his own complicity in the death of Sidney Martin. The act of recalling Martin's death here in more detail allows him to again take thorough control of his fantasy, for the time being. "There were no speed limits. They were beyond the law.... It was exactly as he imagined it" (221). But they are not beyond the law, and Paul Berlin is not beyond his own, internalized set of moral codes. Therefore, just before he moves into the final sprint for Paris, his mind and his memories force him to confront another painful aspect of his time in Vietnam that he has generally avoided until now: the fact that he has been an accessory in the disruption and destruction of the lives of the Vietnamese people.

When Paul Berlin and the others arrive at the seaside, Oscar Johnson, as always, takes charge and arranges in a series of "shady tavern dealings" for their three-day trip from Izmir to Athens (227). Once they are on board the ship en route to Athens, Paul Berlin looks at Sarkin Aung Wan and wonders: "Her own motives were secret. What did she want? Refuge, as sought by refugees, or escape, as sought by victims?" (228). This is followed by their being surrounded by cops and customs agents, and Stink Harris's jumping overboard and vanishing. It is important to keep in mind here, as when reading the Tehran chapters or the chapter where the law is after them in Paris, that these men are guilty of a very real crime. Again, Paul Berlin's journey has been brought to a standstill, and he is about to be faced with another of his unpleasant memories. Immediately after Stink disappears off the coast of Greece, O'Brien

shows him back in Vietnam badgering civilians while Paul
Berlin's squad searches a village. It is in this chapter, "The
Things They Didn't Know," that Paul Berlin attempts to
answer his question about Sarkin Aung Wan's motives and
to confront his own guilt about being a part of the cruelty
and devastation generated by the war.

"The Things They Didn't Know" contains a catalog of
all of Paul Berlin's questions about the Vietnamese people
and his own participation in the war.[12] All of his guilt is
embodied in the questions he asks himself about a "little
girl with gold hoops in her ears" (233). This little girl is the
person from Paul Berlin's memory who provides a model
for the girl who is "maybe twelve, maybe twenty-one" with
"gold hoops through her ears" (48) who accompanies Paul
Berlin on his imaginary trek to Paris—the same girl who
asks him in Paris if she is not too young for him, Sarkin
Aung Wan: "You keep saying I'm a child" (273). As Doc
puts iodine on this little girl's sores, which echoes his
putting iodine on Stink Harris's sores shortly after Sarkin
Aung Wan joins them, Paul Berlin asks himself if she could
"sense his compassion . . . could she somehow separate him
from the war? Could she see him as a scared-silly boy from
Iowa?" (233). These heartfelt questions are followed by
what amounts to Paul Berlin's confessing his guilt about
participating in the war.

In an almost pleading tone, Paul Berlin professes that
he is "innocent. Yes, he was. He was innocent. He would

have told them that, the villagers, if he'd known the
language, if there had been time to talk. He would have told
them he wanted to harm no one. Not even the enemy. He
had no enemies. He had wronged no one" (234). He also
confesses his guilt for allowing "gravity and obligation and
events" to lead him into the war, and he longs to let the
Vietnamese people know that he was not "guilty of wrong
intentions." He even suggests that he might return after the
war and "track down the little girl with gold hoops" and let
her know that he did not go to war "because of strong
convictions, but because he didn't know" (234). Toward
the close of this torrent of sorrow, compassion, and contri-
tion, Paul Berlin says that he will tell this girl what he tells
Sarkin Aung Wan at the end of the novel: "He went to the
war [just as he returns to the war after pursuing Cacciato in
his mind] because it was expected. Because not to go to war
was to risk censure, and to bring embarrassment on his
father and his town" (235). Finally, in what is clearly a state
of great pain and anguish, he says he "would ask her to see
the matter his way. What would *she* have done? What
would *anyone* have done, not knowing?" (235). After Stink
Harris has shot one of Sarkin Aung Wan's water buffaloes,
she asks Lieutenant Corson if they will pay "solace," if they
will pay "reparations" (49). "The Things They Didn't
know" is Paul Berlin's—and, one might add, his creator's—
attempt to offer his words of regret and pain as a scant
payment for his guilt about having served in the war.

GOING AFTER CACCIATO

The narrator says at the close of this chapter that what they *knew* above all else were the "uncertainties never articulated in war stories" (319). Paul Berlin's great task in this novel is to come to terms with the strange blend of uncertainties he experienced in Vietnam by using his imagination to lend enough order and clarity to events so that he can deal with them and at least attempt to understand them. Clearly the United States military was not providing him with the answers he needed.[13] In his closing thoughts on the things they didn't know, he emphasizes that one of the main things of which they were totally ignorant was why America was fighting in Vietnam. He complains that there was no "sense of order or momentum. . . . They did not have a cause" (240).

As this novel unfolds, it becomes increasingly evident that Paul Berlin is trying to cope with a great deal of guilt. In the chapter under discussion, he exposes his immense guilt about being a participant in the war. Previously, he has also shown his confusion about his role in the murder of Sidney Martin and his great shame over his many instances of uncontrolled fear. Paul Berlin has witnessed things he wishes he had not witnessed and done things he wishes he had not done, but the worst part of it all is that none of it seems to have had any meaning. Things have just happened. This is something that torments him throughout the novel, and particularly in the "Things They Didn't Know." It is also a reason why he develops the idea of going after

UNDERSTANDING TIM O'BRIEN

Cacciato. Like the protagonists and narrators of O'Brien's other works, Paul Berlin uses the imagination and storytelling to test his ability to find some order in the things he has experienced and, as far as possible, to make sense of them. The Cacciato story is developed according to a coherent geographic and temporal plan, and despite many crazy episodes, compared to the war, it makes sense. As Paul Berlin chases Cacciato to Paris in his imagination, he discovers that he can organize his experiences into a framework that will lend them some clarity.

Paul Berlin confronts a main source of his guilt and confusion in "The Things They Didn't Know," and he has thus made it possible for the journey to continue. The next chapter, "By a Stretch of the Imagination," opens with his briefly returning to his observation tower to use his imagination to overcome the obstacle of the cops and customs agents in Athens. It closes with Paul Berlin again struggling with the question of why America was fighting the war in Vietnam. The closer he gets to Paris, which is a symbol of western civilization and all of its accomplishments, the more he wonders why such a so thoroughly uncivilized war was fought in Vietnam for over twenty years by two western nations. He philosophizes about the reasons for fighting wars, such as freedom and defending the advances of civilization and promoting "some vision of goodness" (247). He talks about the end coming—"he could feel it" (246)—just as he spoke of it not ending with an arrest at the beginning of the chapter. And as the end nears, he feels "full" of the civilized "desire for order and harmony and justice and quiet" (247). Then, the next chapter opens with a brief battle and the words "Then it ended" (248). It is as if the word "end" in the last chapter had triggered the memory of this scene. Paul Berlin is now at the conclusion of his list of the dead, and he takes one last look at the fruits of civilization: a dead soldier known as Buff, whose face is left stuck in his helmet at the bottom of a ditch, lying in mud, severed from his body. This is the last of the deaths Paul Berlin needs to confront, and it is also the most grotesque.

After O'Brien describes Buff's death, he casually says: "That was all of them" (255). That was the last death and the last of the war stories, and Paul Berlin laments he could not derive any meaningful lessons out of

> those scant hours of horror. . . . Odd, because what he remembered was so trivial, so obvious, so corny, that to speak of it was embarrassing. War stories. That was what remained: a few stupid war stories, hackneyed and unprofound. Even the lessons were commonplace. It hurts to be shot. Dead men are heavy. . . . Scared to death on the field of battle. Life after death. These were hard lessons, true, but they were lessons of ignorance; ignorant men, trite truths. What remained was simple event. The facts, the physical things. A war like any war. No new messages. Stories that began and ended without transition. No developing drama or tension or direction. No order. (255)

Throughout the novel, Paul Berlin has been struggling with the order of events and with the facts, trying to get things straight and constantly asking himself what happened, and where, and when. As he creates the Cacciato story, he provides it with a structured framework, and he gradually learns to do the same with his wartime experiences.[14] He simultaneously summons the courage to confront the "facts." The Cacciato story has furnished him with a way of "asking" and answering "questions" about the war and about himself (27).

In the last "Observation Post" chapter, he talks again of ordering the facts. He goes back over the list of the dead here one more time. He now acknowledges these deaths as facts, and O'Brien tells us: "Those were all facts, and he could face them squarely" (288). He has at least come to terms with this aspect of his war experiences, but he still complains that he has trouble with the "order of facts" and with the "relations among facts . . . It was the trouble of understanding them, keeping them straight" (288). O'Brien equates understanding the facts here with keeping them straight. Ordering the facts thus has something to do with forcing them to somehow make sense. Paul Berlin is not looking for some higher truth in his wartime experiences. O'Brien has already said that the truths derived from war stories are trite.[15] Instead, he is trying to construct a coherent whole out of his wartime experiences so he can at least learn to live with them. He is also trying to figure out how, when and why certain things happened, such as the fragging of Sidney Martin.

The psychologist Jerome Brunner argues that human beings live their lives and "*organize* their experiences and their memories mainly as narrative—stories, excuses, myths, reasons for doing and not doing and so on."[16] O'Brien makes a similar point when he says that everyone does in "one way or another, more or less" (242) what Paul Berlin is doing to get through life. People test various possibilities in their imaginations, tell themselves stories about what they are going to do with their lives, and attempt to lend order to their experiences and memories by narrating them to themselves and others in an acceptable order that can be reached only by being constructed. Brunner also says that narration does not just represent reality but constructs it. And one reason people construct reality out of their memories and experiences is so that they can make sense of them. This is exactly what Paul Berlin does in *Going After Cacciato*. In this novel, Tim O'Brien is exploring the ways in which the creative process can lead to self-knowledge. Paul Berlin develops his idea about going after Cacciato the way "an artist draws out his visions" (24), and like an artist he discovers things about himself as he creates.

As Paul Berlin examines the possibilities of Cacciato's desertion, he comes to terms with his own desire to desert and realizes that he cannot imagine himself as someone who could face the consequences of desertion (286). He knows by the time he reaches Paris in his imagination that in reality he could not endure his family or society censoring him. Simultaneously, as he grapples with the philosophical and moral questions surrounding desertion, he gradually confronts and thinks about the philosophical and moral questions he has about his wartime experiences. In the process, he places them within a narrative framework in which he can examine them. He takes the "facts" of his wartime experiences, which until now have been "separate and haphazard and random" (185), and tries to give them a "real order" (185). The main theme of the novel is thus neither desertion nor the war. *Going After Cacciato* is far more a novel about how people use their memories and imaginations to find order and direction in their lives.

Toward the close of the novel, Paul Berlin wishes he could be through with the whole thing—with the war and with his Cacciato story. "He wanted to go home. A clean bed, his mother and father, the town, everything in its place" (275). Here, too, he is longing for order to replace the chaos and confusion of the war, but this longing for order is also a longing for escape. In the "Observation Post" chapters, however, Paul Berlin uses his imagination to confront rather than to avoid the war and his thoughts of desertion. He has also employed his imagination at other times in his life "as a kind of tool to shape the future. Not exactly daydreams, not exactly fantasies. Just a way of working out the possibilities. Controlling things, directing things" (212).

GOING AFTER CACCIATO

When the reader first meets him, Paul Berlin is so incapable of controlling and directing things that he pees in his pants out of fear. The same thing happens in the last chapter as well. However, the Paul Berlin of the last chapter is not the same person the reader has watched grow throughout this novel. The last chapter is a completion of the novel's first chapter, so that the Paul Berlin who appears in it has not yet created a story about chasing Cacciato to Paris. Paul Berlin is finally able at the end of the novel to confront the complete story of how he lost total control of himself when he and his squad attempted to capture Cacciato because now he *is* more in control of himself.

Early in the story, O'Brien says it was true that "the war scared him silly, but this was something he hoped to bring under control" (57). Paul Berlin's fear has caused him shame during several instances in the novel, and his fear is also probably the main reason he was willing to participate in the fragging of Sidney Martin. But by the end of the novel, Paul Berlin has begun to deal with his fear. He has already confronted many of his moments of fear and shame, and he has started to gain control over his wartime experiences and put them in a manageable order.

Some critics have argued that this novel is about "the struggle and eventual failure to impose order on the flux of experience"[17] or that *Going After Cacciato* demonstrates the "disqualification of the imagination."[18] William Searle even goes as far as to argue there is "no progress, no pattern, no victory, no understanding of an individual's role in the war," a statement that thoroughly disregards such chapters as "The Things They Didn't Know."[19] Such interpretations, however, fail to consider the transformation of Paul Berlin's character as the novel unfolds, or the fact that Sarkin Aung Wan, who argues an entirely different point of view than that of Paul Berlin by the novel's close, is a product of Berlin's imagination.

The Paul Berlin of the Cacciato chapters differs from the Paul Berlin of the war chapters in several ways. For one thing, he takes more initiative, unlike in the war chapters where he appears as a thoroughly passive object. In Mandalay, he tries to capture Cacciato single-handedly. Then later in Tehran, he shows no sign of fear during his imprisonment. Moreover, when he and the others escape from the Iranian prison, he ends up driving the getaway car across the border into Turkey, again while the others sleep. When Paul Berlin and his squad arrive in Paris, he is the first one to step off the train, and during the peace talks as he debates desertion with himself, he is calm and thoroughly in control. In the latter scene O'Brien describes him to us not as a boy but as a mature and thoughtful young man: "His lips, slightly parted, seem on the verge of a shy smile, but his manner is not shy. Reserved, perhaps, but still confident. . . . His hands are steady. His eyes, set wide, are equally steady. No signs of timidity or bashfulness. And when he speaks, leaning into the microphone, his voice is resonant and firm. A diplomat's voice" (285). The changes in Paul Berlin's character toward the end of the novel would not have been possible if he had not already lent some *order* to his wartime experiences and successfully used his imagination to decide what he should do. He can imagine himself doing all of the above things because he has found the courage to confront the war and his role in it.

Throughout the novel, Paul Berlin is extremely concerned with courage: with his own courage, and with whether deserting or staying is the more courageous thing to do. He is also very concerned with what constitutes courage. Of course, O'Brien is also greatly concerned as an author with themes of courage, but nowhere in this novel does he make a definitive statement about individual courage or about Paul Berlin's courage or cowardice. This is typical of O'Brien's method in all of his books. He constantly circles around and around a given theme or idea, but he never conclusively zeroes in on it to offer a final statement. In this novel, O'Brien gradually provides glimpses of Paul Berlin's war experiences, and these fragments slowly come together into stories that lend them order and coherence. Similarly, as the novel unfolds, the reader gets to look at Paul Berlin from many different angles and in many situations. By the end of the novel, Berlin seems more confident, clearer in his thinking and, above all, he seems like a person who has found enough courage in himself to write a book like *Going After Cacciato.*

Notes

1. Robert M. Slabey, "*Going After Cacciato*: Tim O'Brien's Separate Peace," *America Rediscovered: Critical Essays on Literature and Film of the Vietnam War,* ed. Owen W. Gilman, Jr., and Lorrie Smith (New York: Garland, 1990) 206.

2. Tim O'Brien, interview, in *Anything Can Happen: Interviews with Contemporary American Novelists,* ed. Tom LeClair and Larry McCaffery (Urbana: U of Illinois P, 1983) 273.

3. This quote appears on the inside cover page of the 1989 edition of *Going After Cacciato.* See Tim O'Brien, *Going After Cacciato* (New York: Delta, 1989). Subsequent references will be noted in parentheses.

4. Philip Beidler, *American Literature and the Experience of Vietnam* (Athens: U of Georgia P, 1982) 179.

5. Two men from another unit actually did just get up and leave the war: "They just went out and lived and marched from place to place. . . . That was sort of the germ of the narrative of the book." William Hamilton, "Tim O'Brien's Private War with Vietnam," *Boston Globe* 16 May 1978 (*NewsBank,* "Literature," 1978, 9:D8, microfiche). The name Cacciato is an allusion to the Italian verb *cacciare,* which means "to hunt" or "to pursue."

6. Sorting out the "facts" in *Going After Cacciato,* determining "What happened, and what might have happened" (27) can at times be so demanding that some critics even have had trouble getting their facts about the novel straight. For example, G. Thomas Couser writes in his analysis of this novel that Berlin witnesses six deaths, whereas the number is actually eight. See Couser, "*Going After Cacciato*: The Romance and the Real War," *Journal of Narrative Technique* 13 (Winter 1983): 1.

GOING AFTER CACCIATO

Couser also refers to the "search conducted on the train from India to Afghanistan" (5), although this search actually takes place on a train ride from Mandalay to Delhi. Similarly, Robert M. Slabey writes in his critical essay on *Cacciato* that there are nine "Observation Post" chapters, instead of the actual ten, and Milton J. Bates says in his essay on this novel that Paul Berlin is pulling guard duty in a bunker, instead of in a tower. See Slabey 207, and Bates, "Tim O'Brien's Myth of Courage," *Modern Fiction Studies* 33 (Summer 1987): 272. One of the worst misreadings of the text, and one that probably stems from taking what is said in the novel too literally, is Dean McWilliams's labeling Cacciato as "retarded" and "an innocent, contentedly chewing his gum, unaffected by the horrors around him." See McWilliams, "Tim O'Brien's *Going After Cacciato,*" *Critique* 29 (Summer 1988): 250. This statement is clearly contradicted by many of the things Cacciato does and refuses to do in the novel.

      7. Timothy J. Lomperis, *Reading the Wind: The Literature of the Vietnam War: An Interpretative Critique* (Durham: Duke UP, 1989) 46.

      8. It is interesting within this context that O'Brien said in 1983 he thought *The Deer Hunter* was the best of the Vietnam films he had seen up to that time—a movie which is thoroughly immersed in myths about the Old West. See LeClair and McCaffery 267.

      9. The name Sarkin, which is apparently neither Chinese nor Vietnamese, recalls the fictional nation of Sarkin, which is probably meant to be Vietnam, in William J. Lederer and Eugene Burdicks's *The Ugly American.* This character is also O'Brien's version of the female sidekick, Dorothy Lamour, in the "Road"

movies starring Bob Hope and Bing Crosby. Many of the titles of the chapters portraying the imaginary chase to Paris contain a reference to these movies. The first of the imaginary chase chapters is called "The Road to Paris."

10. Tim O'Brien, *Going After Cacciato* (New York: Delacorte, 1978) 84. Subsequent references to this edition will be noted in parentheses.

11. The two "Flights of Imagination" chapters are the only others in the novel—outside of the first and last chapters, both of which are "Going After Cacciato," and the ten chapters called "The Observation Post"—that have the same title.

12. Earlier in the novel, Paul Berlin thinks in an "Observation Post" chapter of going to Paris after the war and learning all he can about the city of his dreams. This is probably in reaction to his sense of ignorance about the foreign country in which he presently finds himself.

13. A marine grunt, quoted in a review of *The Things They Carried,* makes this same point: "They didn't even show us on a map where Vietnam was. We just come over here and started killing'em. We didn't know the history, the language, nothing. They'd pick you up and put you down somewhere and you'd fight for two weeks. Then they'd pick you up and put you down someplace else." Cited in Terry McDermott, "True War Stories," *Seattle Times* 6 May 1990 (*NewsBank,* "Literature," 1990, 12:F9, microfiche).

14. This aspect of the way fiction functions is described by Wolfgang Iser in his new book on the imaginative: "In our ordinary experience, the imaginary tends to manifest itself in a somewhat diffuse manner, in fleeting impressions that defy our

attempts to pin it down in a concrete and stabilized form. The imaginary may suddenly flash before our mind's eye, almost as an arbitrary apparition, only to disappear again or to dissolve into quite another form. 'The peculiar quality of fantasy,' says Husserl, 'is its self-will. And so ideally it distinguishes itself by its absolute arbitrariness.' The act of fictionalizing is therefore not identical to the imaginary with its protean potential. For the fictionalizing act is a guided act. It aims at something that in turn endows the imaginary with an articulate gestalt—a gestalt that differs from the fantasies, projections, daydreams, and other reveries that ordinarily give the imaginary expression in our day-to-day experiences. Here, too, we have an overstepping of limits, as we pass from the diffuse to the precise. Just as the fictionalizing act outstrips the determinacy of the real, so it provides the imaginary with the determinacy that it would not otherwise possess. In doing so, it enables the imaginary to take on an essential quality of the real, for determinacy is a minimal definition of reality." Iser, *The Fictive and the Imaginary: Charting Literary Anthropology* (Baltimore: Johns Hopkins UP, 1993) 3.

15. As in his next book depicting events from the war, *The Things They Carried,* O'Brien is more concerned with the act of telling a war story and with its impact than with its physical, concrete "truth" or factuality. At one point in *Going After Cacciato,* the narrator comments on the veracity of his own story: "People would laugh and shake their heads, nobody would believe a word. Just one more war story" (26). For O'Brien, believing the story does not mean accepting it as factual. Rather, believing the story means *feeling* the significance of what might have happened. For example, when Paul Berlin first encounters

the squalor and poverty of Vietnam, we are told that "He knew what he would see and he saw it. . . . He had seen it all, before seeing it" (226). In reality, he did not actually know the truth about Vietnam until he had spent enough time there to feel in his heart and stomach, as he does in "The Things They Didn't Know," what the war had done to the people and their country.

16. Jerome Brunner, "The Narrative Construction of Reality," *Critical Inquiry* (Autumn 1991): 4–5.

17. Dennis Vannatta, "Theme and Structure in Tim O'Brien's *Going After Cacciato*," *Modern Fiction Studies* 28 (Summer 1982): 244.

18. Arthur M. Saltzman, "The Betrayal of the Imagination: Paul Brodeur's *The Stunt Man* and Tim O'Brien's *Going After Cacciato*," *Critique* 22 (Spring 1980): 36.

19. William J. Searle, "The Vietnam War Novel and the Reviewers," *Journal of American Culture* 4 (1981): 90.

CHAPTER FIVE

The Nuclear Age

Seven years elapsed between the publication of *Going After Cacciato* and Tim O'Brien's next novel, *The Nuclear Age* (1985), a book which according to one critic underwent almost thirty major revisions.[1] At one point, O'Brien apparently discarded his entire first draft and began his novel all over,[2] an action that testifies to his unwavering devotion to what he has often called "getting it right." Unfortunately, despite O'Brien's enormous commitment to this project, the finished product was misunderstood and even attacked by the reviewers. Many of them felt O'Brien should have treated his grave subject of the threat of nuclear war much more seriously than he ostensibly did. For example, one reviewer argues that "O'Brien has grand aims and wants to show how the fear of nuclear holocaust has preyed on the national psyche, and for this he deserves praise. In the end, though, he has written a curiously *little* book about how a high school loser with a nuclear fixation becomes first a college radical with a nuclear fixation and then an adult with a nuclear fixation and nothing more."[3] This reviewer also argues that the book suffers from its "tin-eared dialogue and ridiculous characters." If O'Brien had set out to write a serious exposé of the age of potential mass destruction, then this and similar criticism of the novel for falling short of this task would be legitimate. The fact that he did not, however, means that critics need to reevaluate this novel based on what it actually is as opposed to what many critics wanted it to be.

Almost all of the negative reviews of *The Nuclear Age* contain references to O'Brien's having won the National Book Award for *Going After Cacciato,* and the most negative reviewers all express their disappointment that O'Brien failed to treat the profound subject matter of *The Nuclear Age* as seriously as he did the Vietnam War in his second novel. But O'Brien's third novel is not just about the nuclear age any more than *Cacciato* is just about war. Both novels transcend their subject matter in their relentless emphasis on the human imagination and in their exposure of our human fears of the unknown. In *The Nuclear Age* the modern world provides the backdrop, but as always O'Brien's greatest concern is not with his physical setting but with the way human beings act within this setting. He is interested in the choices people make and in how they use their imaginations and memories to find a way to continue living even under the most awesome and threatening of circumstances.

O'Brien has been criticized for not approaching the threat of nuclear war in his novel with more urgency, but his stated intention was to write a book which read like a "big cartoon of the nuclear age, with everything heightened and exaggerated. . . . It's got kind of a Popeye feel. You know, the muscles are bigger."[4] *The Nuclear Age* is not a "little" book with "ridiculous characters," but an enormously funny book with outrageous characters. It is a satire of an age that has at times been too close to insanity to be treated conventionally. In the tradition of Nathanial West, Tim O'Brien demonstrates in this novel that often the best way to expose a society's inherent madness is to mirror that madness in fiction.

In the 1950s, before the public had fully comprehended the implications of weapons of mass destruction, novels containing horrifying visions of the aftermath of atomic war such as *On the Beach* and *A Canticle for Leibowitz* might have sufficed for forcing people to give more thought to the dangers of the arms race. But for O'Brien, when he wrote *The Nuclear Age* it was no longer enough to attempt to scare people into being reasonable by depicting the imaginary consequences of an atomic Armageddon because "When we decide whether to start a nuclear war we aren't deciding for today; we're deciding for eternity. . . . The nuclear age has changed the terms of our discourse."[5] And, one might add, the existence of large stockpiles of nuclear weapons combined with the tensions of the cold war at the time O'Brien was writing his book called for a new form of fictional representation of the danger of nuclear warfare because the more conventional narratives about this subject suddenly seemed artificial and even trite. Considering the fact that when O'Brien was writing this novel the superpowers were as close as ever to obliterating all of the human values and achievements cultivated over thousands of years, to call nuclear war scary or crazy was a gross understatement—one that O'Brien answers in his novel with an overstatement about the scariness and craziness of a species that can live on a daily basis with the very real possibility of its own extinction.

In *The Nuclear Age,* Tim O'Brien depicts a partially real and a partially imaginary historical period from 1955 to 1995 that he treats as a time in which being crazy is one possible way of staying sane, and sanity as merely the protective covering of utter madness. In light of his approach to his material, it can be argued that even in this novel, O'Brien never leaves his Vietnam experience and the lessons the war taught him about human nature very far behind him. O'Brien portrays the inhabitants of the nuclear age as worthy of Shakespeare's judgment of humankind in *A Midsummer Night's Dream*: "What fools these mortals be." The novel's protagonist and narrator, William Cowling, opens his story with the question "Am I crazy?" After O'Brien's readers travel through more than 300 pages of modern-day adventure, terror, fear, friendship, and love, it should become clear that it is hard for William not to be crazy in an age that bases its notion of sanity on the cool, scientific certainty of thermonuclear physics. *The Nuclear Age* is Tim O'Brien's cartoon-like portrayal of a cartoon age in which the risks involved in simply being alive and trying to live a "normal" life are so great that William Cowling feels he is left with only a few hopelessly crazy alternatives. He can run from the threat of nuclear war. He can try to decrease the possibility of nuclear war through political activism. Or he can choose the Voltairean solution of cultivating his own garden and hope his vegetables will not one day begin to glow after the sun has set. As the story of William Cowling's life unfolds, the reader discovers that for William none of these alternatives makes the madness of the age completely disappear. As William insists throughout the novel, the bombs are real.

O'Brien tells the reader as he begins his story to "just listen."[6] It is April, the year is 1995, and one night shortly after midnight, a forty-nine-year-old man kisses his wife's cheek, slips out of bed, puts on some work clothes, and heads out into the backyard of his luxury home in the Sweetheart Mountains of Montana to begin digging a hole, in which he plans to kill himself and his family. O'Brien asks his readers at the beginning of the novel to close their eyes, "pay attention: Murder, wouldn't you say? A purring electron? Photons, protons? Yes, and the steady hum of a balanced equation." He wants his readers to hear these sounds that have haunted William Cowling most of his life and to perceive William's act of digging a massive hole in his backyard as something sane, as "seizing control."

According to this novel's protagonist, it does not matter whether one digs a hole to escape the bomb, watches

TV and ignores it, or becomes an activist and fights against it. For William Cowling, one thing is certain—in the nuclear age the most important thing one can have is a sense of *security*. O'Brien's third novel is the story of the many crazy, humorous, and often frantic ways that one man tries to find safety in an unsafe world. Ultimately, what William Cowling discovers after he has spent half of his life trying to find protection from the bomb is that being safe involves taking the often dangerous *risk* of admitting there are many things he will probably never know, including when and if the world will end. In this sense, William's fear of the bomb is to a large extent really a fear of the unknown. O'Brien uses the nuclear bomb in this novel as a metaphor for all the unanswered questions human beings have about their existence in a seemingly endless universe.[7]

By the close of the novel, it finally becomes clear to William that it is saner and safer to use one's imagination to find the future than to let one's fear of the unknown dominate one's life. In this sense, *The Nuclear Age* also touches upon a major theme of *Going After Cacciato*. Like Paul Berlin, William Cowling still knows at the end of the novel that he will someday die, but he decides to use his imagination to *believe* otherwise in order to survive the perilous circumstances in which he finds himself. He decides to use his imagination to tell himself stories in which he becomes someone who can summon the *courage* to live in an uncertain world. For William Cowling, as for several of O'Brien's other protagonists, storytelling is thus a form of survival. One of the points this novel makes is that it was the human imagination that envisioned weapons that can annihilate the entire human race, and it is also the imagination that might lead the human race back out of the mess it has created.[8]

When William Cowling goes out into his backyard to dig a hole to escape the threat of nuclear war, it is not the first time he has been forced to do something drastic because of his fear of the bomb. As a twelve-year-old boy, he responded to his nightmares about nuclear war by converting the Ping-Pong table in his basement into a bomb shelter, much to the dismay of his parents: "Maybe it was all that CONELRAD stuff on the radio, tests of the Emergency Broadcast System, pictures of H-bombs in *Life* magazine, strontium 90 in the milk, the times in school when we'd crawl under our desks and cover our heads in practice for the real thing. Or maybe it was rooted deep inside me. In my own inherited fears, in the genes, in a coded conviction that the world wasn't safe for human life" (9). Even when he was a child, William looked for a "sense of security" in an age that made him insecure, and he found it, at least for a moment, in his homemade bomb shelter where he could escape his nightmares of nuclear holocaust and find a peaceful night of sleep.[9] From this point on, his life becomes a relentless search for the kind of relief from his anxieties that he experienced under his Ping-Pong table.

Is William Cowling crazy? Is everyone else crazy? The question of his own sanity becomes vital to him because nobody else seems to *see* the inherent dangers of the age. As he asks at the close of his story, in one of the funniest passages in the novel: "What's wrong with me? Why am I alone? Why is there no panic? Why aren't governments being toppled? Why aren't we in the streets? Why do we tolerate our own extinction? Why do our politicians put warnings on cigarette packs and not on their foreheads? Why don't we scream it? Nuclear war!" (300). While everyone else is busy enjoying the gadgets of the modern world—their televisions and videos and self-cleaning ovens—William Cowling cannot escape his awareness of the most efficient and most modern gadget of them all.

His parents initially respond to his building a bomb shelter in their basement with affectionate irony, but this turns to concern as their inability to take William's fears seriously forces him farther and farther into his obsession with nuclear war. At one point, his mother comes into his bedroom and tries to discover what is really bothering him, since she cannot fathom that it is the bomb alone. He tells her that his sleep is fraught with hallucinations, "weird flashes . . . like lightning, bright zinging flashes" (17). He uses here, as he will elsewhere in the book, his imagination to create an explanation for his own eccentric behavior, mainly because others are incapable of seeing the terrifying things William envisions: "They couldn't understand the real issue—nuclear war and sirens and red alerts—so I had to concoct the flashes as a kind of handle on things, something they could latch on to" (20). This method gets some results, but not the kind William is hoping for. His parents are genuinely worried about the source of his flashes, and so they call in the family doctor, who examines William and decides he is just playing hooky from school. What is worse, after the doctor leaves his room, William can hear him and his parents joking about the Ping-Pong-table bomb shelter. The lesson William learns from this experience, which will become important to him toward the end of the novel, is that grown-up, sane, functional people are too practical to worry about something as abstract as the possibility of nuclear war.

William's childhood fear of the bomb reaches a peak toward the end of the novel's second chapter on the night he has his first full, technicolor vision of nuclear war. His response is to run to the basement and crawl into his bomb shelter, where he begins doubting his own sanity and shouting that he is crazy. His father appears and comforts him with love, words of support, and reassurances, finally convincing him to come out from under the table. As the two of them are moving up the stairs, his father does "a funny thing" and challenges him to a game of Ping-Pong. Out of love for his father, William accepts, and the two of them dismantle the bomb shelter and play "hard" Ping-Pong almost until dawn. The result: "For the next decade my dreams were clean and flashless. The world was stable. The balance of power held" (32). It is significant that William's obsessive fears of the bomb suddenly vanish during the playing of a game, because from here on, it will become increasingly evident that playing games in this novel is a pervasive means of coping with the horrors of the nuclear age. Indeed, a fitting subtitle for this book would have been *The Games People Play.*

After the above events, William settles down and becomes just another kid. He strives to be normal and not stand out, and he succeeds at this until he enters high school, where he begins to withdraw into his own world and become a loner. He is not interested in simply having a good time like everyone else: "I steered clear of parties and pep rallies and all the rah-rah stuff." He views himself as an almost Hamlet-like figure, as someone who thinks too much in a world of people who just want to play games: "I was above it all. A little arrogant, a little belligerent. I despised the whole corrupt high school system: the phys-ed teachers, the jocks, the endless pranks and gossip, the teasing, the tight little self-serving cliques. . . . And who needed it? Who needed homecoming? Who needed cheer-leaders and football proms and giggly-ass majorettes?" (36).

The games the others play are meaningless to him, and so he starts to invent his own distractions. He goes for walks alone in the mountains and collects rocks: "They were safe"

(36). He spends his evenings examining the rocks because it is "reassuring." While the other kids are all out looking for fun and games, William is still seeking the security he had once found under his Ping-Pong table. The bombs are not bothering him, but the world is, and so he cuts it off and withdraws into his own safe cocoon. His parents interrupt his security, however, by putting pressure on him to interact with others, to go out with some girls. He responds to their pressure by using his "greatest asset," his imagination, to come up with at least a temporary solution to this problem.

He begins carrying on fake phone conversations with imaginary friends and girlfriends, as a "parental morale booster," just as he had earlier faked the flashes, a "game, that's all" (37). It was "Safer that way. . . . No Complications. Very clean" (49). However, this game is abruptly interrupted in October of 1962 by the Cuban Missile Crisis and the very real threat of nuclear war. Interestingly enough, William does not panic: "I didn't dream. I felt some fear, of course, but I had the advantage of having been there before, a kind of knowledge" (39). Like so many other Americans during this tense period, who passed the time by "Rolling Dice" or "By playing Solitaire," William and his parents deal with this crisis by waiting and by seeking safety in games: by playing "Scrabble at the kitchen table, quibbling over proper nouns and secondary spellings" (40). And the other kids whom William loathes so much? If they were scared, they didn't show it:

UNDERSTANDING TIM O'BRIEN

There was bravado and squealing.

> *Hey, hey!*
> *What do you say?*
> *Nikita plans*
> *To blow us away.*

A convocation in the school gym. The principal delivered a speech about the need for courage and calm. The pep band played fight songs. Sarah Strouch led us in the Pledge of Allegiance, guileless and solemn, her hand teasing the breast beneath her letter sweater. (39)

Politics are merely a big game in the nuclear age, as William's father suggests (40), and so it is only fitting that the kids at William's school deal with the threat of a nuclear holocaust with which they are confronted in 1962 by treating world politics like a big football game—by writing pep songs, listening to the football pep band play fight songs, and being led in the Pledge of Allegiance by a cheerleader.

During the Cuban Missile Crisis, William remains surprisingly calm, but he suffers from constipation and headaches. Ultimately his parents take him to the doctor for a series of tests. The diagnosis is that his problems are psychological, and so his parents take him to the state capital for a week of psychiatric analysis. During his talks with his analyst—a Mr. Charles, or Chuck, Adamson—it becomes clear and then comforting to William that he is not alone in his hatred of "the whole sports setup in this country" (47), or in his fears of the extinction of the human race. In fact, Adamson seems to be something close to an older carbon copy of William—the reader will not discover until two hundred pages later that this is not altogether true—with the slight variation that William sees the end coming from a nuclear war whereas Adamson believes the natural forces of the universe will destroy the planet.

William Cowling is tormented at various stages in his life by an acute though clearly exaggerated awareness of the possible self-destruction of the human race. He is generally able to cope with this knowledge because his imagination, which allows him to envision a full-scale nuclear war, ultimately enables him to see beyond or around the finite facts. Adamson stresses the importance and the fragility of this gift when he tells William after his own tirade on the end of the human race that imagination is "what you and I have in common. Wonderful faculty, but sometimes it gets out of control, starts rolling downhill, no brakes, and all you can do is hang on for dear life and hope you don't—" (52). What William will learn by the end of the novel is that he can withstand the perils of the age only if he can learn to use his imagination to find a balance in his own mind between the-world-as-it-is, the-world-as-it-might-be, and "the-world-as-it-should-be" (69).

After a week of therapy with Adamson, William is about as "healed" as he will ever be, and so he returns to Fort Derry to complete high school. In 1964, the year it was becoming clear that the American role in Vietnam was going to be something more than merely an advisory one, William leaves home to study at Peverson State College. At college, as in high school, William is a loner, but his studies and his imagination keep him sane. He takes an interest in history and political science, at least in part because he "liked the certainty of absolute uncertainty" (68), a phrase that could be used to describe his fascination with the destructive potential of the nuclear bomb. He also pursues his interest in rocks: "Man was goofy but the earth was tolerant. In geology, there was always time" (69).

He has not been "cured" by his sessions with Chuck Adamson, but he is more capable of carrying on with his life, perhaps because he has found an ally of sorts in Adamson himself. William looks at himself as a "wobbly gyroscope; a normal guy in an abnormal world" (56). Following Adamson's advice, he continues to use his imagination as a kind of companion, sorting out his problems and the world's problems by creating alternatives to reality: "Imagination, that was my chief asset. Not fantasies, exactly, just vivid home movies of the-world-as-it-should-be" (69). He compensates for his failure to do something about the world's problems and the doom he has seen so vividly by imagining himself a mediator between world leaders. Ultimately, he even creates an active love life for himself by indulging in fantasies about Sarah Strouch, the girl to whom he had faked phone calls during high school.

His imagination keeps him sane here, as it does elsewhere in the novel, and it provides him with something in which he can believe: "If we can imagine happiness, we might find it. If we can imagine a peaceful, durable world, a civilized world, then we might someday achieve it. If not, we will not" (70). Unfortunately, the more horrible realities of the world around him are always available as material for his imagination, and so during his second year at college, the bomb drops in on him again. Peverson State College is located on a piece of land on the "banks of the Little Bighorn, ten miles from the famous battlefield, forty miles from SAC's northern missile fields" (67). One night while William is looking out onto the plateau beyond the Little Bighorn, he sees a missile rising, "beyond the football stadium"—a symbol of society's escapist games—and on toward "Canada and the Arctic Ocean, a smooth, graceful parabola that was not without mystique and beauty" (71). William claims that this time, what he sees is the real thing and not a dream, but surprisingly he does not let this ghastly sight bother him. Instead, he calmly turns to his imaginative powers to deal with the problem: "'No sweat,' I said. Imagination, that was my strong suit. I pretended nothing had happened" (71). William responds here to what he believes is a very real missile in the way that most people in the nuclear age deal with such frightening realities—by ignoring it.

William escapes being struck mentally by the missile he sees by imagining it away, but he soon discovers that the powers of his imagination are no match for what he perceives as the overwhelming dangers of the age. The images of chaos and destruction emerging out of the Vietnam War and the domestic protest it generated prey upon William's sanity to the point where his depression and fears cause him to hold a scissors to his throat and briefly contemplate suicide. He responds to this new crisis by picking up the phone and calling Chuck Adamson. Unfortunately, Adamson does not answer his phone, and so William carries on an imaginary conversation with him in which he lists some threats to his peace of mind that he has recently perceived, including the missile he saw and the "disorder" resulting from the war in Vietnam he witnesses on television on a daily basis. In this imaginary conversation, Adamson advises him to "*use*" his "special gift," his imagination, to "figure out what's fact" and what's fantasy (73). From here on, William searches for an acceptable answer to the question of what is the more real, and the more important, fact or fantasy. By the close of the novel, he saves himself by acknowledging that imagining and believing in a happy ending is safer than accepting the end of happiness as a foregone conclusion.

THE NUCLEAR AGE

Whenever William contemplates the horrors of the world around him, he is tormented by the thought that the clear and present dangers he perceives as facts do not generate the type of desperate reaction in others that he experiences. Is he crazy? Is everyone else crazy? The real issue, as William realizes while he is at college, is how much people are willing to *see.* His imagination allows him to envision a full-scale nuclear war, whereas the people around him, the "sane," refuse to recognize even the existence of the bombs themselves. And so, after years of periodic flashes and visions and generally using his imagination to find safety from the bombs, William decides to confront others with the things he can see. He sets up a stand every Monday in front of the college cafeteria, where he holds up a large sign warning people that "THE BOMBS ARE REAL," but still nobody pays attention to him: "The war was real. The technology was real. Even that which could not be seen was real, the unseen future, the unseen letting of unseen blood—and the bombs—the fuses and timers and tickings—and the consequences of reality, the consequences were also real. But no one knew. No one imagined" (75).

William again discovers that most people are incapable of taking his fears and warnings seriously because they are incapable of imagining the realities he can see. For most people, the bombs are not really a danger—they are in fact a "deterrent" to danger. Similarly, the war in Vietnam is not an example of the kinds of horribly wrong miscalculations and mistakes that politicians can make in the nuclear age, but the insane adventure of some insane individuals: "Vietnam, it wasn't evil, it was madness, and we are all innocent by reason of temporary insanity" (131–32). According to William, these things are not real for most people because their reality contradicts the very notion of sane people living in a sane universe: "because none of it was real. If you're sane, that is" (149), "because it's beyond seeing, because we're sane" (150).

In his first serious conversation with Sarah Strouch, William confesses to her about his "crazy" fears and visions. He tells her how it was a matter of "*seeing*" the "Phantom jets and napalm and Kansas burning, how it wasn't a dream, or not quite, or not entirely, just seeing" (93). William sees the threats all too clearly, and he now decides to try to do something about what he sees. He helps organize a zany coalition, the Committee, against the war in Vietnam. He and the other members of the Committee are ultimately forced underground in their protest against the war and their evasion of the draft. As he heads underground, however, just as when he later heads into the ground by digging his hole, it becomes clear that action for William, as for most other inhabitants of the nuclear age, means flight.

He runs from the war, he tells his parents, not out of a sense of "conscience" or "honor," but because "I couldn't envision any other way, because the dangers exceeded the reach of my imagination. Safety, I said. Nothing else" (149). His imagination enables him to see the full horrors of the modern world, but when he sees too much, like many other people he too seeks refuge in an imagined world of normalcy: "it was all a daydream. There are no bombs, I said. We live forever. It's a steady-state universe" (149). Of course, he says this only to console his parents, just as he had earlier concocted the flashes and the fake phone calls to girls to comfort his parents. In reality, William feels more oppressed than ever by the world around him, and so from here on, he chooses escape as a solution to his problems: "it was Trans World" all the way. He plays at being a political activist with the others for a few months, but in essence he does not do much more than run while trying to hide from the realities of the nuclear age. The faster he runs, the clearer it becomes that what William is really unable to face is life and all of its unknown factors.

Whenever William runs, the world always catches up with him. For example, on a TWA flight from New York to Miami, on his way to join the underground movement, he is revisited by a vision of nuclear holocaust. His response is to scoff at this nightmare and find "comfort in knowing it could not be real" (150), but the bombs are real, as William knows all too well. Consequently, although he tries the sane person's trick of denying their reality, his vision—compounded by his sense of despair about being on the run—leaves him physically ill. William spends the next few months recuperating underground at the Committee's hideout in Key West with Sarah and the other members of his new family—Tina, Ned, and Ollie. For the time being, William is safe from the draft and safe from the bomb. Nevertheless, he will soon discover that flight from the nuclear age invariably leads right back into the madness of the age. From the time he takes refuge from the world by heading underground until the time the reader finds him digging his way into the ground in 1995, William becomes increasingly exposed to and a reluctant participant in the mad games people play to survive the threats of the modern world.

Even as a small child, William was shown that the "normal" response to the terrible moments in human history is to treat them as part of a big game. The town in which he grew up, Fort Derry, is not far from the site of one of American history's best examples of the insanity of our species—a small-scale massacre that resulted from full-scale genocide—Custer's Last Stand. Every year the people of the town celebrate this event by crowding into some bleachers and watching it being reenacted, with William's father as Custer being scalped on an annual basis at the celebration's climax. (It is thus no coincidence that William sees his first real, live missile over the banks of the Little Bighorn River.) The novel's second chapter, in which this annual event is first mentioned, is called "Civil Defense." This is an appropriate name for the chapter, mainly because it is in this chapter that William builds his first bomb shelter in response to his nightmares of nuclear war, but also because the celebration of Custer's Last Stand described here is an example of the way people defend themselves against the more unpleasant realities of history—by regarding them as if they were simply part of a big game.

Like the rest of the inhabitants of Fort Derry, William watched history turned into spectacle each year with "fascination" (10), but by the time he is at college, history has become too real for him to treat it as lightly as so many others do. At Peverson State College, he is shown just how shallow people can be in their responses to the historical past and the present. At the height of the Vietnam War, his fellow students stage a carnival in the college gym, to "ward off the midterm blahs" (84), with Custer's Last Stand as its theme. The gym "had been decorated to resemble a large and very gory battlefield . . . with cardboard cutouts of dead horses and burning wagons . . . scalps everywhere—dangling from the basketball hoops, floating in the punch bowl" (84–85). History presented on a basketball court—who could think of a better place to play out what most treat as a game than where games are played? And who would be a better choice for playing Crazy Horse than a football player, a jock, named Ned Rafferty?

Slaughter, mass killings, history, and politics are all one big game in this novel, and a bunch of confused people in a confusing world are the spectators. This is what

O'Brien repeatedly shows a reader in *The Nuclear Age*. William comes to realize that Sarah is right: the terrorism the Committee engages in and politics are like cheerleading: "All that zeal and commitment. A craving for control. A love of pageantry and crowds and slogans and swollen rhetoric. . . . Isn't sex an active ingredient in the political enterprise?" (100). Sex should be fun, politics are a game, though often a dangerous one, and so it is only fitting that Sarah refers to having sex as holding a session of Congress. When it is time for sex, "Congress is in session!"[10]

When the Committee is first formed at Peverson State College, the clownish character Ollie Winckler, who dresses as a cowboy throughout the book, is elected sergeant at arms. This means to him only that he has been assigned a role in a game he enjoys all too well—the potentially destructive game of playing politics: "Jeez, maybe I should get myself an armband or something—I saw that on TV once, they always wear these nifty black armbands" (82). Ironically, by the end of the novel, Ollie will also appear on the magic box where so much of modern-day politics is played out as he and the other remaining members of the Committee are gunned down by government agents at their hideout in Key West (playground for America's jet set) on network TV—more spectacle for the game-hungry inhabitants of the nuclear age. This is how the Committee ends. Characteristically, its first major terrorist act was to disrupt a college football game by turning off the lights on the field.

The sections of the novel that deal with William's participation in the Committee's training and eventual involvement in terrorism make it clear that it is difficult to take
political activity seriously in a world where politics really
are like cheerleading at a big football game. O'Brien shows
the readers of this novel that in an age in which being
politically active is perhaps more important than ever
before, trying to achieve political change can be an absurd
endeavor. Within the anti-war movement, there are "competing factions," as if they were rival football teams, and
fans and participants alike are involved in "cliques and
cabals and petty conspiracies" (158). The two men assigned to prepare the members of the Committee for battle,
Ebeneezer Keezer and Nethro, are right out of a Harold
Pinter play: destruction and murder are a game for them,
one they play with cool precision.

After the Committee members have arrived and settled
in at terrorist boot camp in Cuba, the first thing their
"leaders" do, revealingly enough, is have them practice for
two hours the important skills of standing in silence and
waving. Then they have them play imaginary games of
tennis and volleyball—with no equipment and no nets, but
it is still "Recreation time. . . . Fun an' games" (175). This
is followed by weeks of guerilla warfare training, which
culminates on a night mission to capture and destroy a
wooden tower that Ebeneezer and Nethro have constructed.
Ebeneezer Keezer is a Vietnam veteran, and through the

bizarre training missions he stages, William receives a sufficient dose of what it was like to fight in the senseless war in Vietnam: "If you're sane, you resign yourself to the tacky pleasures of not dying when there is nothing worth dying for" (190).

The night mission in Cuba in which William reluctantly participates is a miniature reenactment of the war in Vietnam, echoing the reenactment of the massacre at the Little Big Horn each year in the town of Fort Derry. Custer's refusal to retreat at the Little Bighorn suggests America's refusal to cry "uncle" in Vietnam and the inability of the inhabitants of the nuclear age to say they have had enough. In this novel, history and politics are nothing more than a game—a spectator sport. Thus, the night mission in Cuba even has a coach, Ebeneezer Keezer, who shouts orders and ridiculous slogans and pep calls through a "bullhorn."

William just wants to live, to save his life and find safety, but no matter which way he turns, the overwhelming threats and insanity of the age are there to meet him. Tim O'Brien once said that all good stories involve a character confronted with making choices:

> I can't think of a story that isn't structured around choices, except maybe for a couple of Flannery O'Connor stories. I'm thinking of "A Good Man Is Hard to Find," which is difficult to talk about in this

way. I mean, who chooses what? Something just happens to those poor people. They go out and they're massacred. Yet what makes the story come alive are the things that those people choose to say and do in the course of this horrible, inexplicable thing. They didn't choose for this to happen to them, but they do choose how to behave as it happens to them.[11]

This statement could also be used to explain William Cowling's predicament in *The Nuclear Age*. William did not choose to live in a world where the equation of science and technology joined by politics equals madness, but reality constantly forces him to choose a course of behavior that will enable him to survive in such a world. Much to his dismay, however, he constantly finds that whether he chooses action or passivity, neither of these alternatives provides him with a means for coping with the insane world in which he lives.

While at college, he chooses a feeble form of action, but he nevertheless does act. His attempt to do something, however, leads him to the heart of the age's craziness when he forms a political committee made up of a bomb-crazy sidewalk cowboy, an overweight girl in white ballet shoes, a cheerleader who just wants to be wanted, and two blood-thirsty clowns. When the war in Vietnam catches up with him, he chooses to run, although he tells his parents that this was not really his decision: "The dynamic decided for me"

(121). As he runs from the senseless war in Vietnam, he gets caught up in an equally crazy war underground. Then, when things in the underground get too out of hand for him, as at so many other times in his life, he indulges in "fantasy" as "a means of escape" (179). However, even in his fantasy he can escape only temporarily, and so somewhere toward the middle of the book, after he has failed his class in terrorist training in Cuba, unlike General Custer, he wisely chooses to retreat. Unlike the other inhabitants of the nuclear age whom O'Brien portrays in the book, William knows when to say *enough*.

Throughout most of *The Nuclear Age* William is like one of the balls that bounced around on the Ping-Pong table he used as a bomb shelter when he was still a child: he is being bounced back and forth into various situations by the giant paddles of the age. When he forms the Committee, for example, he becomes disgusted with the ludicrous behavior and ideas of Ollie and Tina, and he almost abandons the group for good: "The choice was there. . . . A choice, and I chose, but I could've avoided the rest of my life" (84). But after Sarah becomes a team player in the Committee's games, William willingly allows himself to be dragged along for the ride, because of her but also because he believes that the "dynamic" of the age he so often refers to has left him few alternatives. At one point while he is underground, he aptly observes the major difference between Sarah and himself: "Two different value systems. She was out to change the world, I was out to survive it"

(163). Sarah wants to be wanted, and this means putting on a big exhibitionist show in the political arena. William wants to be safe, and this is why his classic gesture, as Sarah puts it, is "to crawl under" his "Ping-Pong table" (172–73).

When the underground starts to get too hot for William, his choice is to seek refuge in his imagination. "Dream time, I decided," and like Paul Berlin in *Going After Cacciato,* he says that he "concentrated" (173) to replace reality with fantasy in order to come to terms with reality. After he fails his course in terrorist training, he spends nine days in a Cuban hospital, withdrawn from the world, fantasizing solutions to its problems. Then he returns to Key West, where William is taken out of action and made a courier for the underground. The historical giant, William the Conqueror, has become the modern-day mouse, William the Cowerer, fleeing odds too great for him to calculate.[12] He becomes a mail pigeon, neither acting for the movement nor acting against it, but merely serving as its passive participant: its Ping-Pong ball. He seeks refuge from the nuclear age by sitting back and taking orders, but the shortcomings of this position become apparent when Sarah and the gang steal a truckload of M16 automatic rifles.

At this point in the novel, William reaches one of his ultimate lows. He is a sweet guy, there is no question about that, but Sarah is right—he is also a jellyfish. He is against the guns and the use of force, but he fails again to take a stand. In the kitchen of the Committee's hideaway in Key

West, the "dynamic" is "at work" (214), but William does not even attempt to stop it. Instead, it is Ned Rafferty who defiantly insists that the guns stay in their crates in the attic, while William serves the others sandwiches: "The price, I was thinking. You play, you pay. I admired him, and I wanted to say something, but it wasn't my game. . . . It wasn't heroism or cowardice. Just noninvolvement: potato chips and coleslaw and iced tea" (218–19). William's earlier response to his fears of the bomb and the violence of the nuclear age was to seek safety, first under his Ping-Pong table and then in rocks. Here he responds to the dangerous game being played in the kitchen by withdrawing into the comfortable security of keeping his mouth shut and serving an All-American lunch.

All William wants is safety and normalcy, but the world offers neither. In their place, there is nothing but games. In one of the most important passages in the novel, O'Brien offers a summary of what William perceives as his principal dilemma. O'Brien also provides his readers with an incisive indictment of the nuclear age:

> It all rang up as tragedy. There were automatic weapons in the attic, and out in the kitchen my colleagues were discussing crimes against the state, but here on the magic box was a contestant in a clown suit squealing over an Amana self-cleaning oven. Where was the rectitude? And where, I mused, did comedy spill over into sadness? Hard to impose

clarity. No theorems, no proofs. Just a war. And the clown-suited contestant bounced and danced in claim of a brand-new self-cleaning oven. Passions were stirred—laughter and greed, the studio audience found it amusing—and Bob Barker rolled his eyes, winningly, as if to absolve: Here it is America, the fruit, the dream, and the price is right.

Happy birthday, I thought. Johnny Olsen's deep baritone: William Cowling—*come* on down!

Curtain Number One: Rio! Cha-cha-cha!

Curtain Number Two: Shine on, William! A trip to the *moooon!* Samsonite luggage and deluxe accommodations along the unspoiled shores of the Sea of Tranquility—Shine on!

Curtain Number Three: Hold tight now, because here it is— You'll never *die!* That's right! Never! A blond stewardess and the northern lights and life ever after. It's all yours . . . iffff the price is right!

But no consolation prizes.

Which made it hard. Risky, choices, and if you guessed wrong the real-life game left you unconsoled. (215–16)

While terror is brewing in the kitchen, William sits and watches a person behaving like a fool over a contemporary symbol of the American dream—something no kitchen should be without—a self-cleaning oven. But as with the self-cleaning device in William's brain, his imagination, the world does not just go away through distractions, games, and the comforts of modern existence. Life involves living, and living involves taking risks, and this is what makes living such a difficult task for him.

In the months that follow the above incident, William continues his work as a courier for the underground movement, until he gets to the point where something in him snaps and he finds himself butchering a snowman he had built in a motel parking lot on New Year's Day 1970: "Stability was a problem. You could only keep running for so long, then the odds caught up and you got mangled like a snowman" (225). It is here that he decides to try action instead of flight, to take a risk and thus take control of his life. For the past few years, William has fantasized about Bobbi, the blond stewardess with whom he fell in love on the flight from New York to Miami just after he had had his last vision of nuclear war. Now he decides to turn his dreams into reality. He uses his greatest asset, his imagination, to create a lasting life for himself—to live with the woman of his dreams "as others live, in fantasy, happily" (226). He takes a risk, the risk of failure, and chooses to go for it: "Curtain Number Three" (228). He employs his imagination, in short, to *create* reality rather than escape it. He attempts to make the future happen by imagining a future instead of imagining none.

Unfortunately for William, when he finally finds Bobbi after a dauntless search, she is married and about to leave for Germany with her new husband. "She was kind about it. She quoted Yeats: *We had fed the heart on fantasies, the heart's grown brutal from the fare"* (232). William's imagination has shown him nuclear war and the end of the world, but it is still his greatest asset because it has also helped him at times to see beyond the end and envision the possibility of a happy and lasting life. Now suddenly, however, his imagination collides with a blank wall: "But it wasn't grief. Not even sadness. If you're crazy, I now understood, you don't feel grief or sadness, you just can't find the future" (232). William's imagination runs dry here, and he cannot picture the future. At the beginning of the novel, the reader finds him digging a hole in his backyard for the same reason. By the end of the book, he has drugged his wife and daughter and carried them into the hole he has dug so he can blow himself up with his family because he can no longer imagine the future. Therein lies a main theme of *The Nuclear Age*: life cannot be lived unless the imagination can find the future "If you're crazy, it's a lapse of imagination. You stare at your dinner plate. You can't generate happy endings. The postulate was obvious. If you're crazy, it's the end of the world" (233). At this point in his life, William is like a storyteller whose creative source of new stories has dried up. He can no longer create a life for himself because he has lost his imaginative gift for telling stories.

After this disappointment with Bobbi, William returns to Key West, and for a few months he just takes things as they come. His imagination is still not working, but he

manages to exist if nothing else. Then one evening, Ned
Rafferty appears in William's room, the two of them talk,
and William tells him everything: about Bobbi, about his
being crazy, about his visions of the bomb and his attitude
toward politics and the underground movement. During his
tirade, he tells Rafferty something that explains much of
what will happen during the rest of the book:

> I told him about obsession and fantasy.
> I told him you had to believe in something: I told
> him how it felt when you stopped believing.
> "It feels fucking crazy," I said, almost yelled,
> then I caught my breath and said, "That's what
> craziness *is*. When you can't believe. Not in anything,
> not in anyone. (234)

William seems close here to putting a scissors to his
own throat again, but by the end of the night, after some
crying and screaming and heavy drinking, he has calmed
down.

Later, William and Ned "borrow" a small boat from the
harbor and spend the night out on the water, talking and
smoking marijuana, "and for a long while I concentrated on
the hemispheres. I watched the scheme of things, the
constellations, the moon veering toward Europe, peace
with honor, Bobbi and Bonn and Rio and Vietnam and the
violet glow of uranium dioxide in the Sweetheart Moun-

tains. I was not afraid. I knew where the future was" (238). As during other difficult moments in his life, William concentrates, an old Paul Berlin trick from *Going After Cacciato,* and his imagination comes back to him. He can again see the future. One of the things he sees is the jewel of the nuclear age—uranium. When he was a youth collecting rocks in the Sweetheart Mountains, he discovered a vein of uranium. Now, at a critical juncture in his life, William's imagination reminds him that he can exploit this discovery to live like he wants—even if the cost of living means supplying the dreaded bomb builders with this magical mineral.

A short time after the night boat ride with Ned Rafferty, William leaves the underground movement. It must be said to his credit that he gets Ned to help him dump the M16 rifles into the ocean before he makes his final break—he is not always a jellyfish. He goes into hiding in the Sweetheart Mountains, where Chuck Adamson helps him find a retreat. William now discovers that Adamson was not the miserable pessimist he had once appeared to be. It turns out, in fact, that Adamson is a happily married man with four children. He is also a master of role reversal, which is the technique he had used to help get William back on his feet a decade earlier.

One thing the Adamson from the earlier encounters does have in common with the real Adamson is a very firm belief in the power of the imagination to shape one's life.

His parting advice to William just before William makes his final break with the underground is to "try to picture the exact circumstances [of the kind of life William wants to lead]. The shapes and routines, the things you want. A blueprint. Then go out and make it happen" (252). Half a decade later, on his thirtieth birthday, William follows this advice and comes out of hiding. Two years later, he enrolls in graduate school: "Geology, it was a natural, and for the next two years I went underground in an entirely new way. I was an adult. I learned about the world we live in, all of us, which was finally a world of real things, sandstone and graphite and plywood and art and books and bombs and the particles that make these things, and how each thing is vulnerable, even Bobbi, who was no longer a fantasy, but real. My dreams were glass. There were no flashes, not even a glow. I was hard and sane" (262).

William has become a citizen of the nuclear age, and an adult. When he was a child and built a bomb shelter under his Ping-Pong table, his parents laughed at him because he used pencils to protect himself from radiation. He thought lead would do the trick, but his parents knew that so-called lead pencils contain graphite and not lead. Now he too can laugh at such things. He is a pragmatist, living in the present and not in dreams and fantasies. He can create his life out of the things of this world rather than out of his imagination. Bobbi is real, and he knows what real thing he can use to get her: uranium!

THE NUCLEAR AGE

By June of 1979, William has completed graduate school, and he spends the rest of the summer in the Sweetheart Mountains deciding what to do about the uranium: "Before me was the rest of my life. What I wanted above all else was to join the world, which was to live and go on living with the knowledge that nothing endures, but to endure. It was a matter of choice. I didn't give a damn about missiles or scruples, all I wanted now was my life, the things of the world, a house and whatever hours there were and the ordinary pleasures of biology. I was hard and sane and practical. I wanted Bobbi, who was real" (262). On New Year's Day 1980, a decade to the day after William had slaughtered the snowman in a hotel parking lot, Sarah and the gang come to visit him. A few months later, the five of them have bought the uranium-rich mountain from a rancher and sold it to the highest bidder. They are now rich—very rich. The cartoon age has produced a group of cartoon millionaires. Tina and Ollie, in his "cowboy hat and fancy boots," return to Key West, where they "would soon be very well-heeled revolutionaries" (269). Ned and Sarah ultimately join them there, but for the time being, Sarah accompanies William in his search for Bobbi, hoping he will not find her. But he does, and the cartoon characters of the nuclear age almost disappear into the sunset—almost.

William and Bobbi settle down in Helena in the hotel he had purchased the day after he cashed his uranium check, and in 1983 they have a daughter. William is now a "real" person; he is practical and functional in a practical and functional world. No more exaggerated, cartoon existence; no more visions. William once told Ned Rafferty that for William's parents, the fact that their son had to go underground to evade the draft was "Like a game. . . . Like it wasn't real" (158). Now he too is an adult, and the problems of the world are just a game. He is sane, and even more important for William, he is safe. He has a real wife, a real daughter, a real life, and he is happy. Nevertheless, the bombs are real too, and after a few years of complacency, tranquility, marital bliss, and meetings at the local Chamber of Commerce, the flashes of nuclear war return to haunt him.

As always, William's response is to run and hide. He builds a house in the Sweetheart Mountains: "It was a large, expensive house, with decks and fine woods and not a neighbor for miles. To be safe, though, I bought up the surrounding land and spent a summer fencing it in. I installed a burglar alarm and dead-bolt locks on all doors" (285–87). Ever since his Ping-Pong table days, William has proven himself an expert at safety. And so when his fortress in the mountains fails to provide sufficient protection and the flashes keep coming, he decides to dig a hole to escape them for good.

Escape is the pattern of the age, and William knows this all too well. In the nuclear age, "we wear alligators on our shirts; we play 3-D video games in darkened living rooms.

... It's an era of disengagement. We are all in retreat, all of us, and there is no going back" (127). Again, he cannot see the future. All his imagination will show him is the end of the world, and so he digs a hole where he can beat the bombs to it—where he can destroy himself and his family before a nuclear holocaust does it for him. As he says in a passage quoted earlier: "If you're crazy, it's a lapse of imagination. ... You can't generate happy endings. ... If you're crazy it's the end of the world" (233). William Cowling follows his instincts when his imagination fails him. He digs because he can no longer imagine an alternative: "The hole is what we have when the imagination fails" (306). Custer in his maddest moment refused to sound the retreat as he watched his world end, but William has been retreating from the madness of the world all of his life.

Toward the close of the novel, just after William has completed his hole, Sarah, who has been dead for several years, returns to him in his imagination. After they have talked for a while about what *might* have become of the two of them under other circumstances, Sarah departs. As she leaves, she tells William, in an almost direct quotation from Brett Ashley's parting words to Jake Barnes at the close of Hemingway's *The Sun Also Rises,* "It's sad that we could've been so happy." However, they could not have been happy because William, like Jake Barnes in Hemingway's novel on an age of desperation, did not have the ability "to see how it could end happily" (252). William followed his imagination when it led him to Bobbi because he could see the future with her. The first time he loses her, he also loses his imagination and thus his ability to see the future. Now, as he prepares to destroy himself and his daughter and wife, his imagination is also gone and he cannot see the future. Bobbi has already left him once since his most recent set of flashes began, and she is about to leave him again, this time for good. This is one of the main reasons why William digs his hole and prepares to end it all. Losing Bobbi means losing the happy ending he envisioned with her.

Imagination dead, imagine. That is the title of one of Samuel Beckett's last books, and it is a phrase that could stand at the top of William Cowling's hole. He has lost his ability to imagine a happy ending and to believe in someone or something. As he tells Ned Rafferty shortly after the first time he loses Bobbi, "That's what craziness *is.* When you can't believe" (234).

His fear of losing his wife and a happy ending to his life is one reason William's flashes return at the end of the novel, but another implicit factor is his possible guilt over the way he made his fortune. His paradise with Bobbi is tentative because it is tainted by radioactively contaminated money. William's flashes of nuclear war can thus also be seen as flashes of remorse. He knows he is guilty of attempting to buy happiness by selling out to the very forces of insanity and apocalypse he fears so greatly, and he has tried to hide this truth from himself. However, as he digs his hole, which reminds the reader of digging for uranium, he ultimately digs free his imagination that his act of hiding from the truth has at least to some extent walled off.

At the end of his story, William Cowling gives his readers an implicitly affirmative answer to the question he raised in his opening sentence about his own sanity. He is unwilling to risk losing Bobbi—he will not "permit separation" (301). Still, as he digs his hole, he digs deeper into himself and realizes, probably more thoroughly than at any other time in his life, that it is better to live with risks than not to live at all. The age in which he lives is fraught with madness and risks because in it, weapons of total destruction are built to deter total destruction. Ultimately, however, William Cowling realizes that it is safer to take risks than to lose the option of taking risks, and it is saner to accept the unknown than to let one's fear of the unknown drive one crazy. He chooses to use his imagination to see beyond the end—to work toward making real a fictional happy ending, and to live with the knowledge that everything will one day end and yet "*believe* otherwise" (312; my italics). Like Paul Berlin in *Going After Cacciato* and Tim O'Brien in O'Brien's next work of fiction, *The Things They Carried,* William Cowling knows that the only way to get a story right is to just keep telling it. O'Brien saved himself from his war memories at least to some extent by confessing about his wartime experiences in his stories in *If I Die in a Combat Zone*. Similarly, Paul Berlin in *Going After Cacciato* deals with his fear during the Vietnam War by telling stories. Tim O'Brien suggests at the close of *The Things They Carried* that he saves his own life by writing stories, and William Cowling also realizes by the end of *The Nuclear Age* that he must continue to use his imagination and storytelling powers to build his life as best he can in a crazy and uncertain world.

Will Bobbi someday leave him? Perhaps. Will the world end in a flash? Possibly. But there is always the chance that things will turn out otherwise: that like Voltaire's Candide, he will be able to cultivate his own garden, and in the nuclear age, this is at least a start. William Cowling chooses to take the risk of living with the things he cannot know, to destroy his hole and save his life and let the mysteries of life lead him on. Who knows, as Tim O'Brien says at the close of the novel, maybe "*E* will somehow not quite equal *mc²*" (312).

Notes

1. Tom Junod, "*The Nuclear Age* Is Noble Effort, But It Fizzles," *Atlanta Journal* 3 Nov. 1985 (*NewsBank,* "Literature," 1985, 14:G7, microfiche).

2. Tim O'Brien revealed this information in an interview with Ruth Bauerle just after the publication of *The Nuclear Age*. See Bauerle, "On the Morality of Nuclear War," *Cleveland Plain*

Dealer 27 Oct. 1985 (*NewsBank,* "Literature," 1985, 12:C7–8, microfiche).

3. Junod, *"The Nuclear Age* Is Noble Effort."

4. Tim O'Brien, interview, in Steven Kaplan, "An Interview with Tim O'Brien," *Missouri Review* 14.3 (1991): 100.

5. O'Brien, in Bauerle, "On the Morality of Nuclear War."

6. Tim O'Brien, *The Nuclear Age* (New York: Knopf, 1985) 3. Subsequent references will be noted in parentheses.

7. This is one of the more subtly placed themes of the novel which many reviewers missed. For example, one critic wrote, mistakenly equating everything William Cowling says with Tim O'Brien's thinking: "O'Brien's most recent work, *The Nuclear Age,* is a warning that our species will not survive if we continue to conceive of the bomb and nuclear war as mere *metaphors.*" Daniel L. Zinn, "Imagining the Real: The Fiction of Tim O'Brien," *Hollins Critic* 23 (June 1986): 2.

8. This is also one of the major premises of H. Bruce Franklin's incisive study of the nuclear age, *Star Wars: The Superweapon and the American Imagination* (New York: Oxford UP, 1988); see esp. 209–10.

9. Tim O'Brien once admitted in an interview that he also built a bomb shelter under his Ping-Pong table as a youth in order to seek protection from the bomb. See Bauerle, "On the Morality of Nuclear War."

10. When asked whether he was trying to make a political statement with *The Nuclear Age,* O'Brien replied: "I don't think I was.... I certainly wasn't trying to. I was trying to write a comedy." Tim O'Brien, interview, in Martin Naparsteck, "An Interview with Tim O'Brien," *Contemporary Literature* 32.1 (1991): 6.

11. O'Brien, in Kaplan 107.

12. Despite William's jellyfish-like behavior at times, he is in O'Brien's eyes the "only hero I've written" because, unlike O'Brien himself, he refuses to serve in Vietnam. William demonstrates the "courage to do what I didn't and a lot of other people didn't, which is to risk embarrassment and censor and endure humiliation by walking away from the war." O'Brien, in Naparsteck 5.

CHAPTER SIX

The Things They Carried

Before America became militarily involved in defending the sovereignty of South Vietnam, it had to, as one historian recently put it, "invent" the country and the political issues at stake there.[1] The Vietnam War was in many ways a wild and terrible work of fiction written by some dangerous and macabre storytellers. First, America decided for Vietnam what constituted good and evil, right and wrong, civilized and uncivilized, freedom and oppression according to American standards; then, the United States military traveled the long physical distance to Vietnam and attempted to make America's notions about these things clear to the Vietnamese people, eventually using brute technological force.

For the American military and government, the Vietnam they had in effect invented became fact. For the soldiers they then sent there, however, the facts their government had created about who the enemy was, what the issues were, and how the war was to be won were quickly overshadowed by a world of uncertainty. Ultimately, trying to stay alive long enough to return home in one piece was the only thing that made any sense at all. As David Halberstram puts it in his novel *One Very Hot Day,* the only fact of which an American soldier in Vietnam could be certain was that "yes was no longer yes, no was no longer no, maybe was more certainly maybe."[2] Almost all Vietnam War writing—fiction and nonfiction—makes clear that the only certain thing during the Vietnam War was that nothing was certain. As Philip Beidler has pointed out, "Most of the time in Vietnam, there were some things that seemed just too terrible and strange to be true and others that were just too terrible and true to be strange."[3]

The main question that Beidler's study of the literature of the war raises is how, considering the overwhelming ambiguity that characterized the Vietnam experience, could any sense or meaning be derived from what happened and, above all, how could this meaning, if it were found, be conveyed to those who had not experienced the war? The answer for Beidler is that "Words are all we have. In the hands of true artists . . . they may yet preserve us against the darkness."[4] Similarly, for Tim O'Brien the language of fiction is the most accurate means for conveying, again as Beidler puts it, "what happened (in Vietnam) . . . what might have happened, what could have happened, what should have happened, and maybe also what can be kept from happening or what can be made to happen."[5] If the experience of Vietnam and its accompanying sense of chaos and confusion can be shown at all, then for Tim O'Brien it will not be in the fictions created by politicians but in the stories told by writers of fiction.

In *The Things They Carried* (1990), Tim O'Brien takes the act of trying to reveal and understand the uncertainties about the war by looking at it through the imagination perhaps a step further than he did in *Going After Cacciato*.[6] In *The Things They Carried,* O'Brien destroys the line dividing fact from fiction, and tries to show even more so than in *Cacciato* that fiction (or the imagined world) can often be truer than fact. As in all of his other works, in *The Things They Carried* Tim O'Brien emphasizes the magical powers of storytelling. He also takes his readers straight into the middle of the process through which facts and memory are transformed in fiction.

The book's first chapter provides a precise account of the items referred to in its title: the things they carried. O'Brien introduces the reader here to some things, both imaginary and concrete, emotional and physical, that the average foot soldier carried through the Vietnamese jungles. O'Brien depicts all of the "things" that appear in the first chapter in a precise, scientific style. The reader is told how much each object weighs, either psychologically or physically, and in the case of artillery, O'Brien even says how many ounces each round weighed: "As PFCs or Spec 4s, most of them were common grunts and carried the standard M-16 gas-operated assault rifle. The weapon weighed 7.5 pounds, 8.2 pounds with its full 20-round magazine. Depending on numerous factors, such as topography and psychology, the riflemen carried anywhere from 12 to 20 magazines, usually in cloth bandoliers, adding on another 8.4 pounds at minimum, 14 pounds at maximum."[7]

UNDERSTANDING TIM O'BRIEN

As this passage shows, even the most insignificant details seem to be worth mentioning. Accordingly, one of the main characters is not just from Oklahoma City but from "Oklahoma City, Oklahoma" (5), as if mentioning the state might somehow make the location more factual, more certain. More striking than this obsession with even the minutest detail, however, is the academic tone that at times makes the narrative sound like a government report. The reader finds, for example, such transitional phrases as "for instance" (5) and "in addition" (7), and whole paragraphs dominated by sentences that begin with "because" (5). O'Brien is striving, above all else, to convince his readers of the importance, the authenticity, of the things they carried.

In the midst of all of this factuality and certainty, however, there are signals that all of the information O'Brien gives the reader in this opening chapter will not amount to much, that the facts are merely there to conceal uncertainties, and that the words that follow the frequent "becauses" do not explain anything. The reader is told in the opening pages, for example, that the most important thing First Lieutenant Jimmy Cross carried were some letters from a girl he loved. The narrator, one of Cross's friends in the war and now a forty-three-year-old writer named Tim O'Brien, tells his readers that the girl does not love Cross, but that he constantly indulges in "hoping" and "pretending" (3) in an effort to turn her imagined love into fact. O'Brien also says "she was a virgin," and then he follows this information with the qualifying remark that Cross "was almost sure" of this (3). On the next page, Cross becomes even more uncertain as he sits at "night and wonder[s] if Martha was a virgin" (4). Shortly after this, Cross wonders who took the pictures he now holds in his hands "because he knew she had boyfriends" (5), but O'Brien never says how Cross "knew" this. Then at the end of the chapter, after one of Cross's men has died because Cross has been too busy thinking of Martha, Cross sits at the bottom of his foxhole crying, not so much for the member of his platoon who has been killed, "but mostly it was for Martha, and for himself, because she belonged to another world, and because she was . . . a poet and a virgin and uninvolved" (17).

This pattern of stating the facts about something and then quickly calling these facts into question that characterizes Jimmy Cross's thoughts in these opening pages is also characteristic of the way the narrator portrays events throughout this book. The facts about an event are given, and then they are quickly qualified or called into question. Then a new set of facts about the same subject emerges, which are again quickly called into question—and on and on, seemingly without end. For example, O'Brien catalogues the various weapons that the soldiers carried, even down to the weapons' weight, thus making them seem important in the sense that their protective power seems real. Several of these passages, however, are introduced by the fact that some of these same weapons were also carried by the character Ted Lavender, and each section of the first chapter (there are four in all) that explains what he carried is introduced by a qualifying phrase that reveals something about which Lavender himself was not at all certain when he was carrying his weapons: he did not know that his weapons would not protect him from ultimately getting shot and killed (4, 7, 10).

O'Brien's method in this book of trying to convey the average soldier's sense of uncertainty about what happened in Vietnam by presenting the "what-ifs" and "maybes" as if they were facts and then calling these facts back into question again, can be seen as a variation of that haunting phrase that was so often used by American soldiers to convey their own uncertainty about what happened in Vietnam: "there it is." Soldiers used this phrase to make the unspeakable and indescribable, the uncertain, very real and present for a fleeting moment. "There it is" would be uttered, for example, to affirm a ludicrous statement made about the horror of the war after someone had been killed. Similarly, O'Brien presents his readers with facts and stories in this book that are certain and real only for a moment because the strange "balance" in Vietnam between "crazy and almost crazy" (20) always creeps back in and forces the mind that is remembering and retelling a story to remember and retell it one more time in a different form, adding different nuances, and then to tell it one more time.

Storytelling in this book is thus something in which "the whole world is rearranged" (39) in an effort to get at the "full truth" (49) about events that themselves deny the possibility of arriving at something called the full, factual truth. By giving the reader facts and then calling those facts into question, and by telling stories and then saying that those stories happened (147), and then that they did not happen (203), and then that they might have happened (204), O'Brien puts even more emphasis in *The Things They Carried* on the question he poses in *Going After Cacciato:* namely, how can a work of fiction paradoxically become more real than the very real events upon which it is based, and how can the confusing experiences of the average soldier in Vietnam be conveyed so that they acquire at least a momentary sense of certainty?

In *The Things They Carried,* the conflict between fact and fiction is made an issue even before the book begins. The first thing to appear at the opening of this book is a reminder that "This is a work of fiction. Except a few details regarding the author's own life, all the incidents, names, and characters are imaginary." Then, immediately after this, O'Brien says that "This book is lovingly dedicated to the men of Alpha Company, and in particular to Jimmy Cross, Norman Bowker, Rat Kiley, Mitchell Sanders, Henry Dobbins, and Kiowa." The six men named here, the reader discovers only a few pages later, are the book's main characters.

These prefatory comments force a reader to consider the fictional as real, since the book is dedicated to the characters who appear in it. O'Brien informs his readers at one point that his intention in telling these war stories is to get at the "full truth" (49) about them, and yet from the outset, he has already shown his readers that the full truth as he sees it is ambiguous: are these stories and their characters real or imaginary, or does the "truth" lie hovering somewhere between the two? A closer look at the book's narrative structure reveals that O'Brien is incapable of answering the questions he initially raises because the very act of writing fiction about the war, of telling war stories, as he practices it in *The Things They Carried,* is determined by the nature of the Vietnam war and ultimately by life where "the only certainty is overwhelming ambiguity" (88).

The emphasis on ambiguity underlying O'Brien's narrative technique in *The Things They Carried* resembles the pattern used by Joseph Conrad's narrator, Marlow, in *Heart of Darkness,* which J. Hillis Miller characterizes as a lifting of veils to reveal a truth that is quickly obscured again by the dropping of a new veil.[8] Repeatedly, O'Brien says that he is telling "the full and exact truth" (181), yet as a reader makes his or her way through the book and gradually finds the same stories being retold with new facts and from a new perspective, it begins to become apparent that there is no such thing for O'Brien as the full and exact truth.

Repeating and varying the same stories in this manner is what O'Brien calls "Good Form" in the title of one of the chapters of *The Things They Carried*. The reason this is good form is that "telling stories" like this "can make things present" (204). The stories in this book are not somehow truer than the things that actually happened in Vietnam because they contain some higher, metaphysical truth: "True war stories do not generalize. They do not indulge in abstractions or analysis" (84). Rather, what makes these stories true is the impact they have as the events within them come alive for a reader. This approach to storytelling echoes Wolfgang Iser's theory of representation in his essay "Representation: A Performative Act." According to Iser,

> Whatever shape or form these various [philosophical or fictional] conceptualizations [of life] may have, their common denominator is the attempt to explain origins. In this respect they close off those very potentialities that literature holds open. Of course literature also springs from the same anthropological need, since it stages what is inaccessible, thus compensating for the impossibility of knowing what it is to be. But literature is not an explanation of origins; it

is a staging of the constant deferment of explanation, which makes the origin explode into its multifariousness.

It is at this point that aesthetic semblance makes its full impact. Representation arises out of and thus entails the removal of difference, whose irremovability transforms representation into a performative act of staging something. This staging is almost infinitely variable, for in contrast to explanations, no single staging could ever remove difference and so explain origin. On the contrary, its very multiplicity facilitates an unending mirroring of what man is, because no mirrored manifestation can ever coincide with our actual being.[9]

From Iser's perspective, when people conceptualize life, they attempt to step outside themselves and look at who they are. And according to Iser, the reason people constantly make new attempts, through telling stories, at conceptualizing their lives and uncovering their true identities is that looking at who they might be is the closest they can to come to discovering who they actually are. Similarly, representing events in fiction is an attempt to understand them by detaching them from the "real world" and placing them in a world that is being staged. In *The Things They Carried,* Tim O'Brien tries to make his readers believe that what they are reading is true because he wants them to step outside their everyday reality and participate in the events he is portraying. It is as if he wants his readers to believe in his stories to the point where they are virtually in them so that they might gain a more thorough understanding of, or feeling for, what is being portrayed in each story. Representation as O'Brien practices it in this book is not a mimetic act but a "game," a process of acting things out, as Iser also calls it in a more recent essay, "The Play of the Text":

> Now since the latter [the text] is fictional, it automatically invokes a convention-governed contract between author and reader indicating that the textual world is to be viewed not as reality but as if it were reality. And so whatever is repeated in the text is not meant to denote the world, but merely a world enacted. This may well repeat an identifiable reality, but it contains one all-important difference: what happens within it is relieved of the consequences inherent in the real world referred to. Hence in disclosing itself, fictionality signalizes that everything is only to be taken as if it were what it seems to be, to be taken—in other words—as play.[10]

In *The Things They Carried,* representation includes staging what might have happened in Vietnam while simultaneously questioning the accuracy and credibility of the narrative act itself. The reader is thus made fully aware of the fact that s/he is being made a participant in a game, in a "performative act," while also being asked to become immediately involved in the incredibly frustrating act of trying to make sense of events that resist understanding. The reader is thus permitted to experience first hand the uncertainty that characterized being in Vietnam. O'Brien forces his readers to "believe" that the only "certainty" was the "overwhelming ambiguity" (79).

This process is nowhere clearer than in a chapter called "How to Tell a True War Story." O'Brien opens this chapter by telling his readers "THIS IS TRUE," and then he wanders through a series of variations of the story about how Curt Lemon stepped on a mine and was blown up into a tree. The only thing true or certain about the story, however, is that it is being constructed and then deconstructed and then reconstructed right in front of the reader. O'Brien gives six different versions of the story of how Curt Lemon was killed, and each version is so discomforting that it is difficult to come up with a more accurate statement to describe his senseless death than "there it is," or as O'Brien puts it in this chapter, "in the end, really there's nothing much to say about a true war story, except maybe 'Oh'" (84).

Before a reader learns how Curt Lemon was killed in this chapter on how to tell a true war story, O'Brien first tells the "true" story that Rat Kiley apparently told to the character/narrator O'Brien about how Kiley wrote to Lemon's sister and "says he loved the guy. He says the guy was his best friend in the world" (76). Two months after Kiley has written this letter, he still has not heard from Lemon's sister, and so he writes her off as a "dumb cooze" (76). This is what happened according to Kiley, and O'Brien assures his readers that the story is "incredibly sad and true" (77). However, when Rat Kiley tells a story in another chapter the reader is warned that he "swore up and down to its truth, although in the end, I'll admit, that doesn't amount to much of a warranty. Among the men in Alpha Company, Rat had a reputation for exaggeration and overstatement, a compulsion to rev up the facts, and for most of us it was normal procedure to discount sixty or seventy percent of anything he had to say" (101).

Rat Kiley is an unreliable narrator, and his facts are always distorted, but this does not affect storytelling truth as far as O'Brien is concerned. The above passage on Rat Kiley's credibility as a storyteller concludes with the statement that "It wasn't a question of deceit. Just the opposite: he wanted to heat up the truth, to make it burn so hot that you would feel exactly what he felt" (101). This summarizes O'Brien's often confusing narrative strategy in *The Things They Carried:* the facts about what actually happened, or whether anything happened at all, are not important. They cannot be important because they themselves are too uncertain, too lost in a world in which certainty has vanished somewhere between the "crazy and almost crazy." The important thing is that any story about the war, any "true war story," must "burn so hot" when it is told that it becomes alive for the listener/reader in the act of its telling.

In Rat Kiley's story about how he wrote to Curt Lemon's sister, for example, the details the reader is initially given are exaggerated to the point where, in keeping with O'Brien's fire metaphor, they begin to heat up. Curt Lemon, according to O'Brien, "would always volunteer for stuff nobody else would volunteer for in a million years" (75). And once Lemon went fishing with a crate of hand grenades, "the funniest thing in world history . . . about twenty zillion dead gook fish" (76). But the story does not get so hot that it burns, it does not become so "incredibly sad and true," as O'Brien puts it, until Rat tells the reader at the story's close that "I write this beautiful fuckin' letter, I slave over it, and what happens? The dumb cooze never writes back" (77). It is these words and not the facts that come before them that make the story true for O'Brien. These words make a reader *feel* Rat's loss and his anger.

At the beginning of this chapter, O'Brien asks his readers several times to "Listen to Rat," to listen more to how he says things than to what he is saying. And of all of the words that stand out in his story, it is the word "cooze" that makes his story come alive. "You can tell a true war story by its absolute and uncompromising allegiance to obscenity and evil" (76). This is just one of the many ways O'Brien gives for determining what constitutes a true war story in an unending list of possibilities that includes reacting to a story with the ambiguous words "Oh" and "There it is." Like these two phrases, Rat Kiley's word "cooze" is an attempt in an unending sequence of attempts to utter some truth about the Vietnam experience and, by extension, about war in general. There is no simplistic moral to be derived from this word, such as that war is obscene or corrupt. "A true war story is never moral. It does not instruct" (76). There is simply the very real and true fact that the closest thing to certainty and truth in a war story as in life is a vague utterance, a punch at the darkness, an attempt to momentarily rip through the veil that repeatedly returns and covers the reality and truth of what actually happened.

It is thus no coincidence that right in the middle of this chapter on writing a true war story, O'Brien says that the main thing he can remember from the short time encompassing Lemon's death, "Even now, at this instant," is Mitchell Sanders's "yo-yo" (83). This toy can be seen as a metaphor for the playful act of narration that O'Brien practices in this book, a game that he plays by necessity. The only real way to tell a true war story, according to O'Brien, is to keep telling it "one more time, patiently, adding and subtracting, making up a few things to get at the real truth" (91), which is ultimately impossible because the real truth, the full truth, as the events themselves, are lost forever in "a great ghostly fog, thick and permanent" (88). The only way to "tell a true war story" is "if you just keep on telling it" (91) because "Absolute occurrence is irrelevant" (89).

"How to Tell a True War Story" ends with the narrator's finally telling how he and Dave Jensen were ordered to climb up into a tree and remove the parts of Curt Lemon's body: "I remember the white bone of an arm. I remember pieces of skin and something wet and yellow that must've been the intestines" (89). He makes six attempts to tell this story before he can finally confront the "truth" as opposed to the mere facts of this story, and the "truth" of the story is that which speaks to a person's heart and stomach: "But what wakes me up twenty years later is Dave Jensen singing 'Lemon Tree' as we threw down the parts." Important in this story, as in all of the stories in the book, is not *what* happened, but what *might have happened.*

Following the narrative technique of this book, a story's truth is clearly not something that can be distinguished or separated from a story, and the veracity or falseness of a story cannot be determined from a perspective outside the story. As Geoffrey Hartman says regarding poetry, "To keep a poem in mind is to keep it there, not to resolve it into available meanings."[11] Similarly, for O'Brien it is not the fact that a story actually happened that makes it true and worth remembering, any more than the story itself can be said to contain a final truth. The important thing is that a story becomes so much a part of the present that "there is nothing to remember except the story" (40). This is why O'Brien's narrator feels compelled to tell and then retell many variations of the same story over and over and over again. This is also why he introduces each new version of a story with such prefatory comments as "This one does it for me. I have told it before many times, many versions but here is what actually happened" (85). What actually happened, the story's truth, is contained in the way the story is told and in how it makes a reader feel—it must take a person beyond the mere facts. A story is true when it entertains, "but entertain in the highest way, entertain your brain and your stomach, and your heart, and your erotic zones, and make you laugh."[12]

There is nothing new in what O'Brien demonstrates here about trying to tell war stories—that the "truths" they contain "are contradictory" (87), elusive, and thus indeterminate. Two hundred years ago, Goethe also reflected on the same inevitable contradictions that arise when one speaks of what happened or might have happened in battle, when he tried to depict the senseless bloodshed during the allied invasion of revolutionary France in his autobiographical book *Campaign in France;* and, of course, Homer's *Iliad* is the primal statement on the contradictions inherent in war. However, what is new in O'Brien's approach to depicting war in *The Things They Carried* is that he makes the axiom that in war "Almost everything is true. Almost nothing is true" (87) the basis for the act of telling a war story.

The narrative strategy that O'Brien uses in this book to portray the uncertainty of what happened in Vietnam is not restricted to depicting war, and O'Brien does not limit it to the war alone. *The Things They Carried* opens, as it closes, with a love story. The book also ends as it begins: with a man thinking of someone he loved in the past. Besides these two women, the reader is also introduced to the Sweetheart of the Song Tra Bong, who is idealized and worshiped as are Martha in the first chapter and Linda in the last. There is also Henry Dobbin's girlfriend, whose nylon stocking continues to protect him even after he learns she has dumped him. In each of these instances, the reader is shown someone conjuring up memories of a person from the past and then telling themselves stories about that person. Moreover, the stories remembered and told in the chapters just mentioned are remembered and told *precisely* to make the present and future bearable and even possible. Storytelling, in short, becomes a means for survival in this book, much as it is in *Going After Cacciato*. When O'Brien tells the story of the death of Curt Lemon, for example, he informs his readers that this story "wasn't a war story. It was a love story" (90). As I said above, there are several other love stories in this book, and I would even argue that this entire book can be seen as a love story. It is O'Brien's expression of his love of storytelling as an act that can wrestle tolerable and meaningful truths from even the most horrible events.

O'Brien concludes his book with a chapter titled "The Lives of the Dead," in which he moves from Vietnam back to when he was nine years old. On the surface, the book's last chapter describes O'Brien's first date, with his first love, a girl named Linda who died of a brain tumor a few months after he had taken her to see the movie "The Man Who Never Was." What this chapter is really about, however, as its title suggests, is how the dead (which can also include people who may never have actually existed) can be given life in a work of fiction. In a story, O'Brien says, "memory and imagination and language combine to make spirits in the head. There is the illusion of aliveness" (260). Like the man who never was in the film of that title, the people that never were except in memories and the imagination can become real or alive, if only for a moment, through the act of storytelling.

When you tell a story, according to O'Brien, "you objectify your own experience. You separate it from yourself" (178). And by doing this, you can externalize "a swirl of memories that might otherwise have ended in paralysis or worse" (179). The storyteller does not, however, just escape from the events and people in a story by placing them on paper. The act of telling a given story is an ongoing and never-ending process. By constantly involving and then reinvolving the reader in the task of determining what "actually" happened in a given situation, in a story, and by forcing the reader to experience the impossibility of ever really knowing with any certainty what actually happened, O'Brien liberates himself from the lonesome responsibility of remembering and trying to understand events. He creates instead a community of individuals immersed in the act of experiencing the uncertainty of all events, regardless of whether these events occurred in Vietnam, in a small town in Minnesota, or somewhere in the reader's own life.

O'Brien thus saves himself, as he says in the last sentence of his book, from the fate of his character, Norman Bowker, who eventually kills himself in a chapter called "Speaking of Courage," because he cannot find some lasting meaning in the horrible things he experienced in Vietnam. O'Brien saves himself in that he demonstrates through the narrative strategy of this book that the most important thing is to be able to recognize and accept the fact that events have no fixed or final meaning and that the only meaning events can have at all is one which momentarily emerges, then shifts and changes each new time they come alive when they are being remembered and portrayed in stories.

Norman Bowker hangs himself in the locker room of the local YMCA after playing basketball with some friends (181), at least partially because he has a story locked up inside himself that he feels he cannot tell because no one would want to hear it. It is the story of how he failed to save his friend Kiowa from drowning in a field of human excrement: "A good war story, he thought, but it was not a war for war stories, not for talk of valor, and nobody in town wanted to know about the stink. They wanted good intentions and good deeds" (169).[13] Bowker's dilemma is thus remarkably similar to that of Hemingway's character Krebs in the story "Soldier's Home." Neither of these men returning from war can tell his story: "At first Krebs . . . did not want to talk about the war at all. Later he felt the need to talk but no one wanted to hear about it. His town had heard too many atrocity stories to be thrilled by actualities."[14]

O'Brien, on the other hand, took on the task after his war "of grabbing people by the shirt and explaining exactly what had happened to" him (179). What he explains in *The Things They Carried* is that it is impossible to know "exactly what had happened." What he wants his readers to know are all the things he/they/we did not know about Vietnam and will probably never know. And what he wants his readers to *feel* in the deepest part of their stomachs is the sense of uncertainty his character/narrator Tim O'Brien experiences twenty years after the war when he returns to the place where his friend Kiowa sank into a "field of shit" and tries to find "something meaningful and right" (212) to say. Ultimately he can only say, "well . . . there it is" (212). Each time a reader of *The Things They Carried* returns to Vietnam through O'Brien's labyrinth of stories, he or she

will become increasingly aware of the fact that this statement is the closest one can probably ever come to knowing
the "real truth," the undying uncertainty of the Vietnam
War.

Notes

1. Loren Baritz, *Backfire: A History of How American
Culture Led Us into Vietnam and Made Us Fight the Way We Did*
(New York: Morrow, 1985) 142–43.

2. David Halberstram, *One Very Hot Day* (New York:
Houghton, 1967) 127.

3. Philip Beidler, *American Literature and the Experience of Vietnam* (Athens: U of Georgia P, 1982) 4.

4. Timothy J. Lomperis, *Reading the Wind: The Literature of the Vietnam War: An Interpretative Critique* (Durham:
Duke UP, 1989) 87.

5. Lomperis 87.

6. The reviewers of *The Things They Carried* are pretty
much split on whether to call it a novel or a collection of short
stories. When I asked Tim O'Brien in an interview in July 1992
what he felt was the most adequate designation, he said that the
book is neither a collection of stories nor a novel: he prefers to call
it simply "a work of fiction." One of the best discussions of the
uniqueness of this book appeared in a review in the *Minneapolis
Star*: "O'Brien is inventing a form here. His book evokes the
hyperintense personal journalism of Michael Herr and the jour-
nalism-as-novel of Norman Mailer, but it is a different animal. It

is fiction, even though its main character has the same name as the author. It is nonfiction, even though Tim O'Brien did not exactly throw the grenade that mangled the slim, dainty young man in black pajamas. It is a confession, but even as he cringes over the doubt and cowardice attributed to Tim O'Brien, the reader must carefully remember Tim O'Brien is a device. . . . *The Things They Carried* defies classification, which won't hurt its survival chances. . . . If I had to label it, I'd call it an epic prose poem of our time, deromanticizing and demystifying and yet singing the beauty and mystery of human life over its screams and explosions, curses and lies." Dan Carpenter, "Author Brings Reality to Vietnam War Story," *Minneapolis Star and Tribune* 12 Mar. 1990 *NewsBank,* "Literature," 1985, microfiche).

7. Tim O'Brien, *The Things They Carried* (Boston: Houghton, 1990) 7. Subsequent references will be noted in parentheses.

8. J. Hillis Miller, "*Heart of Darkness* Revisited," *Heart of Darkness: A Case Study in Contemporary Criticism,* ed. Ross C. Murfin (New York: St. Martin's, 1989) 158.

9. Wolfgang Iser, "Representation: A Performative Act," *Prospecting: From Reader Response to Literary Anthropology* (Baltimore: Johns Hopkins UP, 1989) 245.

10. Iser, "The Play of the Text," *Prospecting* 251.

11. Geoffrey Hartman, *Criticism in the Wilderness: The Study of Literature Today* (New Haven: Yale UP, 1980) 224.

12. Tim O'Brien, interview, in Steven Kaplan, "An Interview with Tim O'Brien," *Missouri Review* 14.3 (1991): 106.

13. In the chapter following "Speaking of Courage," which O'Brien simply calls "Notes," he typically turns the whole

story upside down "in the interest of truth" and tells us that Norman Bowker was not responsible for Kiowa's horrible death: "That part of the story is my own" (182). This phrase could be taken to mean that this part of the story is his own creation or that he was the one responsible for Kiowa's death.

14. Ernest Hemingway, "Soldier's Home," *The Complete Short Stories of Ernest Hemingway* (New York: Scribners, 1953) 145.

CHAPTER SEVEN

In the Lake of the Woods

In *Going After Cacciato, The Nuclear Age,* and *The Things They Carried,* Tim O'Brien focuses on the interaction between memory and imagination, and in each of these books he is concerned with the functions and effects of storytelling. O'Brien shows how people use imagination and stories as instruments for getting through their lives and for contemplating or investigating all of the things they wonder about but will never entirely know. In his latest novel, *In the Lake of the Woods* (1994),[1] O'Brien continues to explore imagination and storytelling, but now from a new angle. He portrays a character who uses magic tricks—both physical and mental ones—as a strategy for survival in an uncertain world. The protagonist, John Wade, has been an amateur magician since his early childhood, and he loves impressing others with his ability to manipulate appearances. Like a good storyteller, Wade is a master at creating illusions.

The novel's first chapter, "How Unhappy They Were," introduces the reader to John Wade and his wife, Kathy. John and Kathy are vacationing in a cabin in northern Minnesota, where they have gone to hide from the world and to salvage what is left of their deteriorating marriage. John has just suffered a devastating defeat in his attempt to win his party's nomination for the United States Senate, and he is grappling with the fact that his stunning political career has come to a sudden halt. During the primary election, Wade's participation in the My Lai massacre in Vietnam was announced by one of his opponents and spread over the front pages of newspapers, thus destroying his campaign. This was a part of Wade's past that he had repressed for close to twenty years. In the novel's opening chapters he is struggling to come to terms with the immense weight of the lost race, the burden of My Lai, and his questionable future. As he attempts in vain to bring his life back into order, he digs deeper and deeper into himself and is confronted with nightmare visions of a life built upon deceit.

John Wade has used his imagination since childhood as a "magical" tool for obtaining some control over reality. It is magical in the sense that it enables him to play tricks in his head and refashion reality to fit his own needs. "At fourteen, when his father died, John did the tricks in his head." He deals with the loss of his father by imagining consoling conversations with him, just as he later does tricks in his head to survive the war in Vietnam. However, like William Cowling in *The Nuclear Age,* Wade knows the imagination has only limited powers, and this scares him. As he admits toward the close of the novel, "the world had its own sneaky little tricks" (251). There are simply too many questions that his imagination cannot answer, such as

IN THE LAKE OF THE WOODS

whether his wife Kathy will ever leave him. He tells her while they are dating in college that he fears their relationship will not last forever, and as he says this he pictures his father's white casket. The casket symbolizes his father's sudden and inexplicable death and thus the unknown, and immediately after he thinks of it he desperately asks Kathy, "but how do we know? People lose each other" (32).

Throughout his relationship with Kathy, John goes through periods of spying on her, trying to know everything about her. His spying, like William Cowling's attempts to control his wife in *The Nuclear Age,* reflects both his fear of the uncertainty of human relations and his desire to have as much control as possible over Kathy and thus over his own future. "The trick then was to make her love him and never stop" (32). Wade's father was an alcoholic whose moods fluctuated frequently, and John could never really be sure about his father's love for him. Consequently, as an adult he tries obsessively to please others and to control as much as possible the way others feel toward him. In his private and public life, like Sarah in *The Nuclear Age,* he just wants to be wanted.

Shortly after John's return from Vietnam in 1969, he and Kathy marry. In keeping with the life he has planned for himself, he completes law school and embarks on a successful political career. He is convinced that he knows where he is going and why. His recent political defeat, however, marks a disastrous failure to please and leaves him thoroughly uncertain about his ability to control and direct his life. His career is a shambles, his marriage is full of tension, and he cannot put his past out of his head—he has successfully made the public disappear by going to the Lake of the Woods, but he has not escaped his own demons. Then, one morning, only a few chapters into the novel, he wakes up and finds Kathy has disappeared. In Vietnam the men in John's squad had called him "Sorcerer" because of his amateur magic tricks, and he had once written to Kathy that he had become the company witch doctor. "Kathy did not write back for several weeks. And then she sent only a postcard: 'A piece of advice. Be careful with the tricks. One of these days you'll make *me* disappear'" (38). Now this warning has become reality, and Wade is left with the task of understanding why she might have left and what his own role might have been in her disappearance.

The spine of the novel in the narrative present consists of John Wade's mental and physical attempts to find his vanished wife. He uses his imagination and memory to learn what might have happened to her and to uncover what her motives might have been for leaving so abruptly. At the same time as he tries to understand Kathy's disappearance, Wade is forced to examine his own distant and immediate past for clues. Did Kathy leave because she could no longer live with all of Wade's deception and manipulation? Did she leave out of fear because of the night she had woken up and found Wade half out of his mind—roaming the house and saying "Kill Jesus" in his rage while pouring boiling water over some house plants? Or did Wade in his night of anguish and derangement kill her and then, in one of his mental magic tricks, repress this act of evil?

As Wade ponders the endless possibilities of what might have become of Kathy, he begins to realize how limited his knowledge of his wife is, despite all of his spying. He also becomes increasingly convinced that she is never going to come back. In fact, the police, the press, and the public ultimately suspect Wade of having murdered his wife because he seems so certain she is gone forever. He is also probably right that she will never return. According to Wade's rather murky recollection of events, Kathy disappeared one late autumn morning in a small outboard motorboat, on a lake that is vast and full of places where one could get lost and never be found. Wade also knows Kathy had plenty of reasons for disappearing. The two of them had always been deeply in love, but John put his career over his marriage for close to twenty years and, as a result, he gradually lost touch with Kathy's needs and expectations. Out of her great love for him she had played the game of climbing the political ladder along with him and being a good politician's wife, but by the time of her disappearance she was at a point where their estrangement had reached a new height. For almost a month Wade joins the massive search for her, but in the end he begins to believe that the only way he will ever find her is also to disappear into the

Lake of the Woods—which is what he does toward the novel's close.

While John Wade is searching for his wife, the narrator also involves his readers in his own obsessive search for the reasons why Kathleen Wade, and ultimately John Wade, disappear. O'Brien's narrator thus also plays the role of a detective—in the great tradition of Marlow in Conrad's *Lord Jim* and the reporter figure in Orson Wells' *Citizen Kane*. The narrator is never given a name in the novel but, like the narrator with the name of Tim O'Brien in *The Things They Carried,* he should not be equated with the novel's author Tim O'Brien—although this distinction becomes blurred in some of the novel's footnotes. The structure and style of the novel are designed to support and underline the narrator's act of investigating the disappearance of Kathleen and John Wade at the Lake of the Woods in northern Minnesota. Much of the book is written as an elaborate missing person's report—complete with detailed footnotes, pieces of evidence, and many excerpts from personal interviews. In a footnote the narrator refers to the book's chapters as "notebooks" (103), as if the chapters were part of an investigative report instead of pieces of a work of fiction; and in another footnote we learn how the narrator, true to his role as an investigator, traveled all the way to the site of the My Lai massacre in Vietnam "in the course of research for this book" (149).

Like all of O'Brien's writings, this novel is structured around a very deliberate and complex arrangement of chapters. There are seven "Evidence" chapters; seven "Hypothesis" chapters; several chapters with titles containing the words *who, what,* or *where,* in the tradition of crime fiction; and chapters addressing compelling and mysterious issues, with titles such as "The Nature of Loss" and "The Nature of Love." Even more than in his other works of fiction, however, the tightly ordered structure in this book is constantly shattered by O'Brien's insistence on the mystery of the unordered and indeterminate universe in which we live.

The importance of the unknown and the unknowable in this novel is reflected in the way O'Brien counteracts his systematic documentation of the double disappearance with a form of writing that is almost impressionistic. As in a montage film, the reader of this text is overwhelmed with a mosaic of images and thoughts that constantly undermine one another and open new possibilities regarding Kathy and John Wade's disappearance. As the novel moves slowly from the disappearance of Kathy Wade to the final vanishing act of John Wade, cause and effect becomes a doubtful idea in the wake of a flood of contradictory statements about Wade and his wife. In addition to this, in the evidence and hypothesis chapters the narrator constantly reminds his readers that facts and truths are subject to the laws of relativity.

In the novel's seven hypothesis chapters the narrator tries to understand Kathy Wade's motives and desires, and to explain her sudden disappearance by entering her mind.

He attempts to imaginatively reconstruct why Kathy might have left and what might have happened to her. In the process he also probes John Wade's psyche, trying to understand his behavior as well, even as Wade pursues his own quest—both inward and outward—for his absent wife. In this search to discover where Wade's wife—and ultimately Wade himself—might have gone and why, the narrator does what most people do when they try to understand others: he develops a hypothesis, looks at the empirical evidence, and then uses his imagination to try to gain at least partial knowledge of what he admits he will never entirely know—the remote regions of his subjects' hearts and minds.

The narrator's mental and physical journey after Kathy and John Wade resembles Paul Berlin's imaginary pursuit of Cacciato in *Going After Cacciato*. As he uses his imagination to understand their thoughts and actions, and to contemplate what might have become of them, the narrator's investigation triggers memories of his own lost past. In this way his investigation has the cathartic effect of helping him retrieve part of his own "vanished life" (301), which at such moments seems to blend together with Tim O'Brien's "lost" life. In this sense O'Brien's novel about the search for Kathy and John Wade is a search for self, and an attempt to understand his own role as a fiction writer and storyteller.

IN THE LAKE OF THE WOODS

Like all of his other writings, this novel reflects on fiction writing and storytelling as an act of exploration—all of O'Brien's fiction to date explores the mysterious recesses of the human heart and the limits of human consciousness. The narrator refers to himself in a footnote as a "theory man" (30) mainly because he practices storytelling in this novel as an attempt to construct imaginative theories of what might happen to human beings under a given set of circumstances. Simultaneously he exposes fiction writing itself as a form of spying, where the writer attempts to penetrate the innermost regions of the personalities or spirits of other human beings.

As in *Going After Cacciato* and *The Things They Carried,* O'Brien in this novel seems more concerned with what might have happened than with what actually did happen. Potentiality takes precedence over actuality because in fiction—as in life—explanations about human behavior lead to new questions. While the narrator is bombarding his readers with an assortment of evidence and facts, he constantly reminds them that facts are tentative at best and evidence can only tell us what is apparent. "Even much of what might appear to be fact in this narrative—action, word, thought—must ultimately be viewed as a diligent but still imaginative reconstruction of events" (30).

As he retells the story of the double disappearance, the narrator provides his readers with quotes and references taken from every imaginable source—including interviews the investigating narrator held with those who knew or searched for Kathy and John Wade. He also refers to books written about the My Lai massacre, psychoanalytic studies of major political figures, and an array of important literary works. Like a good detective, the narrator seeks out as much supporting evidence as possible to prove his case. Paradoxically, however, what he ultimately demonstrates is that certain human matters—such as those of the heart and soul—can never be fully explained. The more evidence one obtains in an effort to explain such issues as love and loss and spirit, the more one is confronted with the endless possibilities for alternate explanations. "It's conjecture—maybe this, maybe that—but conjecture is all we have" (53).

O'Brien's emphasis on the tentative nature of human knowledge is supported by the novel's style. The tone and style of the evidence chapters are relatively flat, which has led some critics to overlook their important function in the book's total design and to dismiss them as aesthetically damaging to the book's impact.[3] These are the chapters that contain the "documented" evidence the narrator has gathered during his research, and one of their functions in the novel is to underline the seriousness of his attempt to get at the facts. The hypothesis chapters, on the other hand, contain some of O'Brien's most powerful prose and storytelling. They thus overshadow the evidence chapters through their artistic superiority. In this way O'Brien subtly influences his readers to choose conjecture over fact and to prefer the possibilities of stories over supposedly "factual" data. Of course, even the facts in the evidence chapters must be seen ultimately as stemming from conjecture, because the statements and quotes appearing in these chapters are based on subjective opinions and perceptions. And, finally, both "evidence" and "hypothesis" are fictional products of the author O'Brien's imagination.

When the narrator writes as a "Biographer, historian, storyteller, medium," after having gathered evidence over "four years of hard labor," he still admits that he is "left with little more than supposition and possibility" (30). This is because in the end the only heart and soul he can even come close to truly penetrating—according to this novel—is his own. "We find truth inside or not at all" (298). O'Brien illustrates the absolute limits of the human ability to understand oneself and others through the story of John Wade's incapacity to gain full knowledge of himself or Kathy—and, ultimately, through his narrator's inability to solve the mystery of John and Kathy's lives.

Since early childhood, John Wade has looked upon magic as a means for controlling and comprehending the world around him. "As a boy John Wade spent hours practicing his moves in front of the old stand-up mirror down in the basement. . . . In the mirror, where miracles happened, John was no longer a lonely little kid. He had sovereignty over the world. Quick and graceful, his hands did things ordinary hands could not do. . . . Everything was possible, even happiness" (65). Magic helps him cope with his father's cruelty when he is drunk. He even develops a trick for making his father stop drinking. And just as O'Brien reaches into his own bag of tricks as a fiction writer in his attempt to penetrate the soul of his protagonist, John Wade often employs his imagination in this novel to understand the people in his life.

Wade spies on his father—as the writer spies into the private sphere of his characters' lives—for the same reason he later spies on Kathy: to bring under control the things about his father he does not understand. "Everybody had secrets, obviously, including his father, and for John Wade the spying was like an elaborate detective game, a way of crawling into his father's mind and spending some time there. He'd inspect the scenery, poke around for clues" (214). His spying, like his fascination with magic, is part of his extreme need to gain control of the world around him. Similarly, spying on his wife "opened up a hidden world, new angles and new perspectives" (33). Spying, like magic, "gave him some small authority over his life" (213).

Until the moment when his political career collapses, Wade firmly believes in his magical ability to direct and control his life. When the men in his squad in Vietnam nicknamed him Sorcerer he wrote to Kathy that "I sort of like it. Gives me this zingy charged-up feeling, this special power or something, like I'm really in control of things" (61). John's fellow soldiers looked on him as something of a good-luck charm. When at one point his luck seemed to have faded, during an ugly period of ambushes and mine explosions, he soon retrieved his status by walking up to a Vietcong sniper who had just killed a squad member and shooting him in the face. "The little man's cheekbone was gone. Afterward, the men in Charlie Company couldn't stop talking about Sorcerer's new trick" (40) of making the sniper's cheekbone "disappear." Such "magic" tricks give him the self-confidence he otherwise lacks—mainly as the result of his father's ambivalent behavior toward him.

Wade enjoys the thrill of using his magic to manipulate, at least temporarily, the restraints of cause and effect. He is thus fascinated by Vietnam, which provides a special challenge to the magician in John Wade. He "was in his element. It [Vietnam] was a place with secret trapdoors and tunnels and underground chambers . . . a place where the air itself was both reality and illusion, where anything might instantly become anything else. . . . The war itself was a mystery. . . . Secrecy was paramount. Secrecy *was* the war" (73). It was a place where, for a while at least, John Wade could convince others he had "certain powers, certain rare skills and aptitudes" (37). In Vietnam, like later during his political career, Wade proves himself a great role player. He "encouraged the mystique" of being the company sorcerer because it brought him admiration and a sense of belonging (38). In Vietnam, where superstition helped mitigate the fear, Wade became a good-luck charm.

Wade in essence hides behind his sorcerer's mask in Vietnam and projects an image of himself as someone who can uniquely manipulate the "hows and whys." However, as the narrator says when he struggles in vain to explain the horror of My Lai, "It was the sunlight. It was the wickedness that soaks into your blood and slowly heats up and begins to boil. Frustration, partly. Rage, partly. . . . But it went beyond that. Something more mysterious. The smell of incense, maybe. The unknown, the unknowable. The blank faces. The overwhelming otherness. This is not to justify what occurred on March 16, 1968, for in my view such justifications are both futile and outrageous. Rather, it's to bear witness to the mystery of evil" (203). When Wade is confronted with this side of Vietnam during the My Lai massacre, his magic fails him and he is overcome by the absolute evil that the "otherness" of Vietnam exposes in himself and in his fellow soldiers. He feels himself being pulled like a dead spirit through the wasteland of My Lai (40), just as later in his life when his traumatic past catches up with him his campaign manager describes him as resembling a "walking dead man" (102).

My Lai reveals the potential darkness of the human heart to John Wade—a darkness so terrifying that he runs from it rather than confront it. This is the turning point in his life. He is given the opportunity to expose the evil in which he participated and to admit that there are mysteries over which he has no control. But this would involve confession, and "the notion of confession felt odd. No trapdoors, no secret wires" (218). Instead of confronting himself and his own participation in evil, he turns to his magic to erase the mysteries. First he "tricked himself into believing" that a murder he committed in My Lai "hadn't happened the way it happened," believing he could "fool the world and himself too" (68). Then he takes advantage of the clerk's position he receives during his final months in Vietnam and changes his records, transforming himself into a soldier with an honorable and warcrime-free record (272).

Wade tries to atone for the sins he committed in My Lai by extending his stay in Vietnam. "He needed to reclaim his own virtue. At times he went out of his way to confront hazard, walking point or leading night patrols, which were acts of erasure, a means of burying one great horror under the weight of many smaller horrors. Sometimes the trick almost worked. Sometimes he almost forgot" (150–51). Similarly, over the next two decades he tries to exorcise the ghosts of My Lai by being a successful politician and believing that in this way he can do some good and improve the world. Nevertheless, My Lai will ultimately prove to Wade that coming to terms with himself and his past requires more than a quick hand. Just as Paul Berlin in *Going After Cacciato* never fully escapes in his imagination his participation in the murder of Lt. Sidney Martin, John Wade's magical rewriting of his war records does not save him from his memories of My Lai. Nor does it provide a guarantee that the image he creates of himself after the war as an idealistic politician will not someday be shattered.

The narrator repeatedly shows in the evidence chapters, through an assortment of references to the personalities and motives of major political figures, how politicians create an image of themselves by performing various roles for the public in their almost obsessive need to be liked. Politics is thus the perfect career choice for Wade, who is a master at manipulating images. "Early on, with practice, he cultivated an aspect of shyness in his public demeanor, a boyish quality that inspired trust" (155). He also "cultivated—Sincerity. He worked on his posture, his gestures, his trademark style. Manipulation, that was still the fun of it" (155).

Wade's campaign manager, Tony Carbo, points out a main motive behind Wade's political ambitions when he says, in an evidence chapter, that "politics and magic were almost the same thing for him. Transformations—that's part of it—trying to change things. When you think about it, magicians and politicians are basically control freaks" (27). The narrator confirms this assessment of Wade's character when he later writes "Power: that was the thing about magic" (71). This is also an idea that Wade himself had already read about as a boy in *The Magician's Handbook:* "The capacity to do what is manifestly impossible will give you a considerable feeling of personal power" (28).

Even before he went to Vietnam, John Wade had fixed his eyes on a political career and had managed to convince Kathy that his intentions were purely altruistic. The narrator, however, exposes Wade's deeper motives by pointing out that, as with most everything else, control was his ultimate goal. "He had the sequence mapped out; he knew what he wanted. . . . He talked [to Kathy] about leading a good life, doing things for the world. Yet even as he spoke, John realized he was not telling the full truth. Politics *was* manipulation. Like a magic show: invisible wires and secret trapdoors" (34–35). By the time he returns from Vietnam his need to exert control over his life and manipulate the impression others have of him has reached a new height.

During the two decades following the war, Wade becomes an absolute master of deception. He convinces his wife that his heart is pure, to the point where she refuses to listen to Tony Carbo, who sees Wade as being primarily a cynical manipulator of images. During a discussion with Wade about his political career, Carbo offers an accurate assessment of this man who refused to expose the evil of My Lai: "Anyhow, don't pin that ruthless crap on me. Things go wrong, man, I pity the poor fucker gets in your way. Real honest-to-God pity" (166). That Kathy will not listen to Carbo's rejection of the image Wade has created of himself as a "dreamer" is ironic, since this conversation takes place shortly after Wade has persuaded his wife to abort the baby she so badly wants because it would be an obstacle to his career plans.

Even after his participation in the My Lai massacre has been exposed, following what is probably Wade's most surrealistic night of disorientation and madness since the war, and just prior to his discovery of Kathy's disappearance, he still believes he can "prove to her that he was back in control. A solid citizen. Upright and virtuous" (79). In the end, however, as indicated above, his magical attempt to recreate himself catches up with him.

> He'd tried to pull off a trick that couldn't be done, which was to remake himself, to vanish what was past and replace it with things good and new. He should have known better. Should've lifted it out of the act. Never given the fucking show in the first place. Pitiful, he thought. And no one gave a shit about the pressure of it all. Twenty years' worth. Smiling and making love and eating breakfast and keeping up the patter and pushing away the nightmares and trying to invent a respectable little life for himself. The intent was never evil. Deceit, maybe, but the intent was purely virtuous.

IN THE LAKE OF THE WOODS

No one knew. Obviously no one cared.

A liar and a cheat.

Which was the risk.

You had to live inside your tricks. You had to be Sorcerer. Believe or fail. And for twenty years he had believed.

Now it ends, he thought.

One more fucker with no cards up his sleeve. (238)

Just prior to his own disappearance, Wade finally admits to himself that knowing oneself goes beyond believing in the image one has created for others.

O'Brien uses the story of John and Kathy Wade to explore significant existential questions: How well does one really know oneself? Who really are the people with whom one interacts? And how well does one ever get to know the person one marries? To what extent can such questions even be answered? John Wade had a wife he greatly loved and who loved and believed in him. He also had a promising political career with a large constituency of voters, voters who had accepted the image he projected of himself. Then, in one sweep, he loses everything because something terrible from his past suddenly surfaces. The identity he has created for himself and others, selectively using his memory and imagination, is abruptly destroyed. He has spent his life trying to control both it and the world around him with his magic, spying, and manipulation, and once again, as at My Lai, his magic is failing him.

John Wade's ability to control or manipulate his reality breaks down at two important junctures in the novel: during the My Lai Massacre and on the night before his wife leaves him. In both instances he becomes thoroughly disoriented and acts almost involuntarily, as if he no longer knows who he is or what he is doing. On the night before Kathy leaves, "The unities of time and space had unraveled. There were manifold uncertainties, and in the days and weeks to come, memory would play devilish little tricks on him. The mirrors would warp up; there would be odd folds and creases; clarity would be at a premium" (51). As a politician he had neatly planned his life and career, and had tricked the world into believing in a contrived image. Now, however, he is paying the price for avoiding self-knowledge. He has run out of tricks for deceiving himself and others, and he is left with a void where he once had a neatly packaged self-image—a carefully planned life.

Tim O'Brien has his narrator investigate the heart and soul of John Wade to illustrate the limits of self-knowledge and the impenetrability of otherness.

What drives me on, I realize, is a craving to force entry into another heart, to trick the tumblers of natural law, to perform miracles of knowing. It's human nature. We are fascinated, all of us, by the implacable otherness of others. And we wish to penetrate by hypothesis, by daydream, by scientific investigation those leaden walls that encase the human spirit, that define it and guard it and hold it forever inaccessible. . . . Our lovers, our husbands, our wives, our fathers, our gods—they are all beyond us. (103)

Nevertheless, at the very moment the narrator admits that in the end he is incapable of discovering any final truths about other people, he leaps back into his investigation of the disappearance of Kathy and John Wade because, as he says in a passage quoted earlier, conjecture is all we have and "mystery itself carries me on" (269). The unquenchable desire of human beings to obtain knowledge of things unknown is, according to this novel, potentially one of the most uplifting characteristics of the human spirit. As the narrator suggests at one point, it is the fascination with enigmas and a hunger to solve the mysteries of the universe that leads the species to create religions and erect great temples (269). O'Brien's emphasis on exploration as a goal of fiction writing supports this idea.

In the evidence chapters of his novel, O'Brien shows his readers the repeated attempts of those who knew the Wades or were familiar with their story to solve the mystery of what happened to them. As Kathy's sister at one point complains, people seem "obsessed" with the story of John and Kathy Wade (194). This kind of obsession can be simply vulgar curiosity, such as when people wonder about the victims of an accident. But the human obsession with the unknown or unknowable, according to O'Brien, can also lead to great acts of imagination and courage. O'Brien shows in his story of John Wade both extremes of this equation.

If John Wade killed his wife, perhaps out of frustration because he could not penetrate her soul enough to know if she would ever leave him, then his imagination failed him in the worst possible way and he is indeed a "monster" (306). The novel contains theories by such cynics as Vinny the cop, who seems to enjoy believing Wade brutally killed his wife. The narrator says that he rejects this version of the story's ending, but he admits that the ending one chooses is a matter of taste and "there's no accounting for taste" (303). On the other hand, if Wade actually pulled off what the narrator suggests would have been Wade's ultimate trick, and joined his soul with Kathy's—by also disappearing into the endless mystery of the Lake of the Woods—then in some strange way he really was a great magician, and his fascination with secrets and manipulation led him on to create an unsolvable and intriguing mystery.

At one point in the novel, Wade tells his wife that she is not behaving like herself, and his campaign manager responds to Wade's remark by pointing out that Kathy has multiple identities. "And which *you* is that? Seems to me she's got yous galore. Yous here, yous there" (225). The full weight of this question does not become apparent to Wade until it is too late and Kathy has disappeared. His wife's disappearance without any clues leaves Wade in a position where he gradually begins to accept that he never really knew her. Simultaneously, he is confronted with his own delusions about himself and his marriage. Out of these ashes, however, O'Brien grants his protagonist one more shot at the "grand finale," the ending Wade so desires. He lets John Wade disappear and become an eternal mystery. He also permits Wade at least a partial chance to redeem himself—in the tradition of Fitzgerald's Gatsby—by suggesting that Wade might have nobly sacrificed himself to an ideal: to love.

This novel, like O'Brien's previous four books, is also a love story. "A grand finale, a curtain closer. He did not know the technique yet, or the hidden mechanism, but in his mind's eye he could see a man and a woman swallowing each other up like that pair of snakes along the trail near Pinkville, first the tails, then the heads, both of them finally disappearing forever inside each other. Not a footprint, not a single clue. Purely gone—the trick of his life" (76). This is what might have happened, and O'Brien seems to favor this ending. He changed the novel's closing paragraphs in his final version of the text to emphasize the immensity of John's love for Kathy as he is about to disappear forever aboard a small motorboat somewhere on the Lake of the Woods. "The throttle was at full power. He was declaiming to the wind—her name, his love" (306).[4] The novel's closing stress on Wade's longing for his wife strongly suggests that his last trick was to fulfill his dream of suturing his life together with hers—at least in his mind.

Perhaps even more than in *The Things They Carried,* O'Brien shows in this novel that in stories, as in life, there are no definite conclusions. O'Brien tries at one point to give his story a happy ending, "But truth won't allow it. Because there *is* no end, happy or otherwise. Nothing is fixed, nothing is solved. The facts, such as they are, finally spin off into the void of things missing, the inconclusiveness of conclusion. Mystery finally claims us" (304). O'Brien holds true to this thought by constantly emphasizing at the close of his novel the inconclusiveness of John and Kathy Wade's story. What became of them is left to conjecture, and O'Brien leaves it up to each reader of this novel to choose an appropriate ending. The novel thus closes with a question mark, true to O'Brien's notion that otherness is in the end impenetrable.

The indeterminate ending of this novel represents O'Brien's acknowledgment of the limitations of the fiction writer's power to construct reality to suit his or our needs and desires. In the final version of his text, O'Brien also adds a statement to the passage just quoted which gives another reason why this story must remain an eternal mystery. "The ambiguity may be dissatisfying, even irritating, but this is a love story. There is no tidiness. Blame it on the human heart" (304). The question mark at the end of the novel is the same question mark Wade comes up against at the end of his quest to understand himself and others. As O'Brien suggests in the novel's closing pages, maybe life for John Wade the storyteller and magician was also nothing more than a massive puzzle.

In the Lake of the Woods synthesizes the themes and concerns of all of O'Brien's prior works. It also reveals, possibly more than any of his other books, O'Brien's fascination with the existential struggle to come to terms with the unknown quality of life and otherness. The reader is told that before John married Kathy, he used to spy on her in an attempt to know everything about her: "The issue wasn't trust or distrust. The whole *world* worked by subterfuge and the will to believe" (33). The one certainty about the world in O'Brien's fiction is that it is an uncertain place.

Vietnam taught Tim O'Brien that people never totally know themselves or those around them. People select what they want to know and remember about themselves based on who they imagine they are, but there is always the possibility that some major event will arise that will force them to call their self-image into question. There is always the potential for something like the Vietnam War to enter people's lives and shock them into a recognition that they can never completely know who they really are. The last chapter of *If I Die in a Combat Zone* is titled, "Don't I know you?" O'Brien learned in Vietnam that self-knowledge and one's knowledge of others is always limited. He also learned that there is a great potential for evil and self-deception in most human beings. Most people want to believe they are decent and kind, but as Joseph Conrad also suggested, no one is altogether free from the grips of the heart of darkness.

Notes

1. In a phone interview that I held with O'Brien about one year before this novel was published, he told me he planned on naming it *The People We Marry*. The novel's original title emphasized the mystery of otherness. The final title switches the emphasis to the mysterious nature of human knowledge.

2. Tim O'Brien, *In the Lake of the Woods* (Boston: Houghton Mifflin, 1994) 31. All subsequent references will be noted in parentheses.

3. This thinking can be found, for example, in the first review of the novel by Sybil S. Steinberg in *Publishers Weekly* (11 July 1994: 61).

4. O'Brien also added to his final manuscript a long passage emphasizing Wade's love for his wife which does not appear in the advance preview copy of the book, distributed about four months before the book's actual publication. The closing pages of the final version of the novel also suggest far more than the preview copy that Wade was probably not responsible, at least physically, for Kathy's disappearance.

BIBLIOGRAPHY

Books by Tim O'Brien

If I Die in a Combat Zone, Box Me Up and Ship Me Home. New York: Delacorte, 1973; London: Calder, 1973; New York: Delta, 1989 (revised edition).

Northern Lights. New York: Dell, 1975; London: Calder, 1975.

Going After Cacciato. New York: Delacorte, 1978; London: Cape, 1978; New York: Delta, 1989 (revised edition).

The Nuclear Age. New York: Knopf, 1985.

The Things They Carried. Boston: Houghton Mifflin, 1990.

In the Lake of the Woods. Boston: Houghton Mifflin, 1994.

Selected Short Fiction and Excerpts from O'Brien's Novels

"Claudia Mae's Wedding Day." *Redbook* 141 (Oct. 1973): 102–3.

"Keeping Watch by Night." *Redbook* 148 (Dec. 1976): 65–67.

"A Man of Melancholy Disposition." *Ploughshares* 2.2 (1976): 46–60.

"Quantum Jumps." *Ploughshares* 9.4 (1982): 11–44. Rpt. in *The Pushcart Prize, X: Best of the Small Presses,*

BIBLIOGRAPHY

1985–86. Ed. Bill Henderson. Wainscott, N.Y.: Pushcart, 1985. 3–31.

"The People We Marry." *Atlantic Monthly* 269 (Jan. 1992):
90–92, 94, 97–98.

"Loon Point." *Esquire* Jan. 1993: 90–94.

Selected Essays and Other Nonfiction by O'Brien

"All Quiet on the Western Front." *TV Guide* 10 Nov. 1979:
19–20.

"The Ballad of Gary G." *New York Magazine* 15 Oct. 1979:
67–68. Review of *The Executioner's Song,* by Norman
Mailer.

"Burning Love." *Saturday Review* 27 Oct. 1979: 41–42.
Review of *Endless Love,* by Scott Spencer.

"Darkness on the Edge of Town." *Feature* 38 (Jan. 1979):
42–49.

"Reporter of ABC Springs News Leak on U.S. Supreme
Court Actions." *Los Angeles Times* 20 Apr. 1979, sec.
1: 18.

"Falling Star." *Saturday Review* 17 Feb. 1979: 53–54.
Review *Incandescence,* by Craig Nova.

"Flying High." *Saturday Review* 10 June 1978: 37–38.
Review of *Airships,* by Barry Hannah.

"Honor Thy Commander." *Saturday Review* 16 Feb. 1980:
50. Review of *A Game Men Play,* by Vance Bourjaily.

BIBLIOGRAPHY

"Revolt on the Turnpike." *Penthouse* Sept. 1974: 62–64, 147–48, 156–60.

"Simplistic Demagogy." *Washington Post* 23 Oct. 1973: B6.

"The Vietnam Veteran—The GI Bill: Less Than Enough." *Penthouse* Nov. 1974: 76–78, 128, 142–45.

"The Vietnam Veteran—Prisoner of Peace." *Penthouse* Mar. 1974: 44–46, 61–62, 64, 113–17.

"The Violent Vet." *Esquire* Dec. 1979: 96–97, 99–100, 103–4.

"We've Adjusted Too Well." *The Wounded Generation: America After Vietnam.* Ed. A. D. Horne. Englewood Cliffs, N.J.: Prentice, 1981. 205–7.

"What We Talk About When We Talk About Love." *Chicago Tribune: Bookworld* 5 Apr. 1981: 1–2. Review of *What We Talk About When We Talk About Love,* by Raymond Carver.

Interviews with O'Brien

"Author Tim O'Brien Interviewed." *Los Angeles Times* 25 Nov. 1979: 3.

Bauerle, Ruth. "On the Morality of Nuclear War." *Cleveland Plain Dealer* 27 Oct. 1985. *NewsBank,* "Literature," 1985. 12:C7–8. Microfiche.

Blades, John. "War Stories." *Chicago Tribune* 27 Apr. 1990, sec. 5: 1–2.

BIBLIOGRAPHY

Carlson, Peter. "Famed Author's Lot: Kisses and Kicks." *Herald American* 26 May 1979, sec. 4: 3.

Kaplan, Steven. "An Interview with Tim O'Brien." *Missouri Review* 14.3 (1991): 93–108.

LeClair, Thomas, and Larry McCaffery, eds. *Anything Can Happen: Interviews with Contemporary American Novelists.* Urbana: U of Illinois P, 1983. 262–78.

Naparsteck, Martin. "An Interview with Tim O'Brien." *Contemporary Literature* 32.1 (1991): 1–11.

Schroeder, Eric James. "Two Interviews: Talks with Tim O'Brien and Robert Stone." *Modern Fiction Studies* 33 (Summer 1987): 135–51.

Selected Articles and Book Chapters about O'Brien

Allen, Bruce. "Survival on the Slopes." *Newsday* 4 Jan. 1976. *NewsBank,* "Literature," 1976, 2:B5, microfiche.

Baritz, Loren. *Backfire: A History of How American Culture Led Us into Vietnam and Made Us Fight the Way We Did.* New York: Morrow, 1985.

Bates, Milton J. "Tim O'Brien's Myth of Courage." *Modern Fiction Studies* 33 (Summer 1987): 263–79. Discusses the uniqueness of O'Brien's notion of courage in terms of its being more philosophical and more civilized than that of most other writers of war fiction.

Beidler, Philip D. *American Literature and the Experience of Vietnam.* Athens: U of Georgia P, 1982. Chapters on

BIBLIOGRAPHY

Going After Cacciato and *If I Die in a Combat Zone*. Treats both books as attempts to wrestle some meaning out of the war experience. Contains some excellent insights.

Brunner, Jerome. "The Narrative Construction of Reality." *Critical Inquiry* (Autumn 1991): 4–5.

Calloway, Catherine E. "Pluralities of Vision: *Going After Cacciato* and Tim O'Brien's Short Fiction." *America Rediscovered: Critical Essays on Literature and Film of the Vietnam War*. Ed. Owen W. Gilman, Jr., and Lorrie Smith. New York: Garland, 1990. 213–24. Looks at the problematic nature of what constitutes reality in *Going After Cacciato* and interprets the subjective nature of perception in this novel. Also contains some illuminating comparisons of sections of the novel with excerpts that were first published in magazines as short stories.

Couser, G. Thomas. "*Going After Cacciato*: The Romance and the Real War." *Journal of Narrative Technique* 13 (Winter 1983): 1–10. Analyzes the novel's style and structure as part of O'Brien's attempt to find an adequate way of portraying the war and concludes that, as in romance narratives, O'Brien is forced by his subject to raise rather than resolve the most disturbing questions about the war.

Dowling, Tom. "The Endless March of War." Review of *The Things They Carried,* by Tim O'Brien. *San Francisco Examiner* 5 Apr. 1990. *NewsBank,* "Literature," 1990, 5:B9, microfiche.

BIBLIOGRAPHY

Gilbert, Marc Jason, ed. *The Vietnam War: Teaching Approaches and Resources.* New York: Greenwood, 1991. Several articles in this book make reference to O'Brien's fiction and discuss strategies for teaching his Vietnam texts.

Griffith, James. "A Walk Through History: Tim O'Brien's *Going After Cacciato.*" *War, Literature, and the Arts* 3 (Spring 1991): 1–34. Examines the novel and its historical context.

Halberstram, David. *One Very Hot Day.* New York: Houghton, 1967.

Hamilton, William. "Tim O'Brien's Private War with Vietnam." *Boston Globe* 16 May 1978. *NewsBank,* "Literature," 1978, 9:D8, microfiche.

Herzog, Tobey C. "*Going After Cacciato:* The Soldier-Author-Character Seeking Control." *Critique* 24 (Winter 1983): 88–96. Stresses Paul Berlin's attempt to order his Vietnam experiences by creating the Cacciato story.

Jones, Dale W. "The Vietnam of Michael Herr and Tim O'Brien: Tales of Disintegration and Integration." *Canadian Review of American Studies* 13 (Winter 1982): 309–20. Compares Michael Herr's approach to depicting the war in *Dispatches* to O'Brien's in *If I Die in a Combat Zone* and concludes that O'Brien was more capable of transcending the insanity and violence of Vietnam.

BIBLIOGRAPHY

Junod, Tom. "*The Nuclear Age* Is Noble Effort, But It Fizzles." *Atlanta Journal* 3 Nov. 1985. *NewsBank,* "Literature," 1985, 14:G7, microfiche.

Lomperis, Timothy J. *Reading the Wind: The Literature of the Vietnam War: An Interpretative Critique.* Durham: Duke UP, 1987. Contains some excellent observations about O'Brien's works by other Vietnam War writers. Interspersed throughout the text are O'Brien's comments about the war and the literature it generated.

McDermott, Terry. "True War Stories." *Seattle Times* 6 May 1990. *NewsBank,* "Literature," 1990, 12:F9, microfiche.

McWilliams, Dean. "Time in Tim O'Brien's *Going After Cacciato.*" *Critique* 29 (Summer 1988): 245–55. Provides a helpful sequential and chronological breakdown of the novel. Discusses the novel's structure in terms of Paul Berlin's efforts to deal with his wartime memories.

Mehren, Elizabeth. "Short War Stories." Review of *The Things They Carried,* by Tim O'Brien. *Los Angeles Times* 11 Mar. 1990. *NewsBank,* "Literature," 1990, 4:B3, microfiche.

Myers, Thomas Robert. *Walking Point: American Narratives of Vietnam.* New York: Oxford UP, 1988. Insightfully examines *If I Die in a Combat Zone* within the context of other personal narratives on the Vietnam War. Emphasizes O'Brien's approach to courage and his ambiguous and confused relationship to tradition.

BIBLIOGRAPHY

Nelson, Marie. "Two Consciences: A Reading of Tim O'Brien's Vietnam Trilogy: *If I Die in a Combat Zone, Going After Cacciato,* and *Northern Lights*." *Third Force Psychology and the Study of Literature.* Ed. Bernard J. Paris, Rutherford, N.J.: Fairleigh Dickinson UP, 1986. 262–79. Treats all three books as part of a trilogy which depicts O'Brien's struggle to overcome his "authoritarian conscience" and learn to live with his "humanitarian conscience."

Raymond, Michael W. "Imagined Responses to Vietnam: Tim O'Brien's *Going After Cacciato*." *Critique* 24 (Winter 1983): 97–104. Emphasizes the role of the imagination and fantasy but does not deal adequately with the importance of fear in the novel.

Saltzman, Arthur M. "The Betrayal of the Imagination: Paul Brodeur's *The Stunt Man* and Tim O'Brien's *Going After Cacciato*." *Critique* 22 (Spring 1980): 32–38. Accuses O'Brien of betraying the imagination but fails to take into account the fact that at the close of the novel, O'Brien gives two versions—Paul Berlin's and Sarkin Aung Wan's—of what the imagination can create.

Searle, William J. *Search and Clear: Critical Responses to Selected Literature and Films of the Vietnam War.* Bowling Green State UP, 1988. Contains some valuable insights into the structure of *If I Die in a Combat Zone* and *Going After Cacciato.*

BIBLIOGRAPHY

Searle, William J. "The Vietnam War Novel and the Reviewers." *Journal of American Culture* 4 (1981): 90.

Slabey, Robert M. "*Going After Cacciato*: Tim O'Brien's Separate Peace." *America Rediscovered: Critical Essays on Literature and Film of the Vietnam War*. Ed. Owen W. Gilman, Jr., and Lorrie Smith. New York: Garland, 1990. 205–12. Examines O'Brien's development in *Going After Cacciato* of a new technique of writing in his attempt to portray the Vietnam War.

Smith, Lorrie. "Disarming the War Story." *America Rediscovered: Critical Essays on Literature and Film of the Vietnam War*. Ed. Owen W. Gilman, Jr., and Lorrie Smith. New York: Garland, 1990. 87–99. Insightfully examines conventional war fiction and demonstrates how O'Brien breaks with tradition in his books on the Vietnam War.

Vannatta, Dennis. "Theme and Structure in Tim O'Brien's *Going After Cacciato*." *Modern Fiction Studies* 28 (Summer 1982): 242–46.

Wiedemann, Barbara. "American War Novels: Strategies for Survival." *War and Peace: Perspectives in the Nuclear Age*. Ed. Ulrich Goebel and Otto Nelson. Lubbock: Texas Technological UP, 1988. 137–44. Treats Paul Berlin's fantasy in *Going After Cacciato* as a means of preserving his sanity under the insanity of the war. Not very in-depth. Discusses *Going After Cacciato* in terms

of what the article's author labels Paul Berlin's unsuccessful attempt to use the imagination to impose order on
the flux experience.

Wilhelm, Albert E. "Ballad Allusions in Tim O'Brien's
'Where Have You Gone, Charming Billy?'" *Studies in
Short Fiction* 28 (Spring 1991): 218–22. Illuminatingly
analyzes musical allusions in sections of *The Things
They Carried.*

Woods, James. "Words of War." *Minneapolis Star and
Tribune* 10 Mar. 1990. *NewsBank,* "Literature," 1990,
5:B8–9, microfiche.

Zinn, Daniel L. "Imagining the Real: The Fiction of Tim
O'Brien." *Hollins Critic* 23 (June 1986): 1–12. Ana-
lyzes the contrast between the imaginary and the real in
Going After Cacciato, Northern Lights, and *The Nuclear
Age* and criticizes O'Brien for not being more polemical
about his subject matter in *The Nuclear Age.*

Bibliography

Calloway, Catherine. "Tim O'Brien: A Checklist." *Bulle-
tin of Bibliography* 48.1 (1991): 6–10.

Biographical Source

Baughman, Ronald, ed. "Tim O'Brien." *Dictionary of Literary Biography Documentary Series: American Writers of
the Vietnam War.* Detroit: Bruccoli, 1991. 137–214.

BIBLIOGRAPHY

Audio-visual Materials

Going After Cacciato. Seven audiotapes. Read by John MacDonald. Books on Tape, 1985.

Tim O'Brien. Audiotape. A discussion of O'Brien's life and works, recorded at Macalaster College, St. Paul, Minn., 1981.

The Things They Carried. (Abridged.) Two audiotapes. Read by Anthony Heald. Harper-Audio, 1991.

The Things They Carried. Videotape. Read by Tim O'Brien at Radford University in Radford, Va., 20 Nov. 1991. Telecommunications Bureau, 1991. 47 min.

INDEX

INDEX